Award-winning comedian Jeff Green is one of the most popular comics working in the UK today. He has staged several sell-out tours in the West End and throughout Britain and Australia. He appears regularly on television and radio, and has starred in several TV specials of his own. His previous two books, *The A–Z of Living Together* and *The A–Z of Being Single*, were both bestsellers. He lives in London with his partner and baby.

Also by Jeff Green in Sphere

The A–Z of Living Together
The A–Z of Being Single

JEFF GREEN

The A–Z of Having a Baby

A Survival Guide

sphere

SPHERE

First published in Great Britain in 2006 by Sphere
Reprinted in 2006 (twice)

A CIP catalogue record for this book is available from the British Library.

ISBN 978-0-7515-3688-1

www.littlebrown.co.uk

For my parents

'If you want to experience the pain of child birth, take your bottom lip, and pull it over your head'

CAROL BURNETT

'I know as men, we'll never get to experience the true majesty that is childbirth but then, we can open all our own jars'

ME

Introduction

Congratulations. You're having a baby!

As a soon-to-be parent, no doubt you have hundreds of questions running through your mind: Is it a boy or a girl? Will it have ten fingers and toes? Will it be Prime Minister or Pope (always best to aim high)? Pop idol or chartered accountant? Is it mine or that bastard's from down the road who keeps smirking at me in the post office? Where's the best church to abandon it if it turns out to be one of the horrible whiny ones you see in supermarkets and motorway service stations, jacked up on Sunny Delight with a foot of toxic green mucus hanging from its nose? How do I childproof my stereo? OK, calm down. One at a time.

So what brought you to this fantastic, life-affirming, bank-account-draining, figure-ruining predicament?

Maybe you lost your sense of rhythm at the critical moment.

Maybe the condom fell off.

Maybe you got fed up with your life of order, wealth and calm and fancied having all your favourite stuff covered in snot and jam for the next few years.

Perhaps you've just given up smoking and will go to any length for a puff on a cigar.

Maybe you wanted women to smile at you in the park again.

Maybe you're on income support, and, feeling obliged to conform to your stereotype, have just squeezed out your thirteenth in ten years.

Maybe you wanted to get on aeroplanes before anyone else.

Maybe you actually planned it.

Who knows?

Whatever the reason, I don't doubt that fear (yes), uncertainty (definitely) and elation (optional), as well the odd bout of piles (mandatory), are all struggling inside you and giving you grief as we speak.

If you are a man, I'm sure you will be viewing your partner with undisguised awe, armed with the newly gained knowledge that compared to the miracle that your partner is going through, your once proudly held skills of oiling squeaky doors and bleeding radiators are now looking pretty pathetic.

If you are a woman, I'm sure you will be viewing your partner with undisguised contempt, struggling with your newfound knowledge that although he has expressed undying love for you, it is that tricky little bastard who got you into this beaver-splitting mess in the first place.

One thing is certain – your world will *never* be the same again. There are words and phrases you will use in the next twenty years that you have probably never used in the previous twenty – your child's name, for example. There are others too: 'Get down from there', 'Put it back!', 'Give me some peace', 'Please let go of my eyebrows', '*How* much?' and, of course, 'Oooh, smelly'.

Expectant parents may be wondering when to start acting like a mum or dad. For men, the earlier the better. Why not try sneaking in a few 'dad' things for practice? You could wear tracksuit bottoms with shoes, for example, or you could start dancing badly at parties or stopping every time you spot a good piece of wood in a rubbish skip ('Ooh, I could use that wood').

Mums-to-be might want to get in some early training by spitting on a hankie and smearing it on the face of a passing midget, setting aside a pair of *good* scissors for no one to touch, or you could just dunk your breasts in a saucer of milk (T-shirt still on of course) for that 'new mum' look.

So who will gain from reading this book? Well, if you're *planning* on becoming pregnant then reading this book might help you appreciate that you are not alone and that it might not be too late to nip to the chemist, get a gross of condoms, a prescription for Nordette and slip on some garlic-laced knickers with a picture of Ann Widdecombe on the front. If you *are* pregnant – and assuming you're pleased with the idea – this book will help illuminate the road you are about to travel, so that you don't tread in so much caca (of which there is much). If you've already *been* pregnant (and have received a knock on the head thus rendering the whole experience forgotten – it happens) then hopefully this book will be a pleasant reminder of all the fun and pain (oops, there's the p-word, and we're only on the second page) coming your way again.

If you have teenagers, you might want to buy this book, leave it on their pillow and hope they might start concentrating in maths rather than on the opposite sex, and save you all a lot of grief. It could also give you an unexpected appreciation for any menopausal flushes you might be experiencing.

Where this new baby/pregnancy book differs from most others is that it is penned from a man's point of view. *What the hell does a man know about having a baby?* you may ask. As little as we can get away with without losing cuddling rights, I reply, which is probably why this book should be invaluable – in these days of modern parenting, the more a man knows, the better it is for everyone, especially Mum. It might also mean that leaving the baby with Dad is not the gamble it used to be: '*You gave him a bacon sandwich, at three weeks?*' After all, you can't hand *this* one back when its eyes cross, its face turns puce and a vague smell of rotten bananas fills the room. It's yours for life!

You are taking the first, albeit scary, steps on what is life's most amazing journey – parenthood. The only journey no one ever regrets – have you ever met someone who says: 'I wish I never had him', apart from maybe Mr and Mrs Bin Laden? I hope this book helps shine a little laughter into your lives at a time of joy, trepidation and complete strangers prodding you on buses. I'd better go now, there's a rather disturbing noise coming from somewhere that I can't place – it's a mixture of panic and ecstasy. Is it the radio? The TV? No, wait. It seems to be coming from my throat.

Good luck, to all three of you.

Jeff Green

The A–Z of Having a Baby

A

Abilities (above average) (*see also* Pushy Parent syndrome, etc.)

Once your baby arrives, it is perfectly natural to want to brag about it, everyone does. However, besides pushy fathers, mothers are also notoriously competitive with other mums when it comes to their children's abilities:

SHE: He clapped along to 'Twinkle, Twinkle, Little Star' today.

FRIEND: That's great. Although my boy did that last month. Now he's moved on to playing the Rumba note perfect on my boobs each morning.

YOU: John Constable's *Hay Wain* is a wonderful painting.

FRIEND: It is, although I have to say my child's collage of a snowman in cotton wool and macaroni is technically much better.

FRIEND: My daughter's very good at sculpture.

YOU: Yes, but she does insist on using her own poo.

FRIEND: That's NOT important.

The fact is you don't need to gild the lily as far as your offspring are concerned. Babies *are* clever, but not in the ways you might think. OK, they can't say what they want *exactly,* and their nose-wiping skills leave a lot to be desired, but when you've sat down to eat a meal (several house walls away!) they can tell instantly and will let you know they've sussed you by letting out a healthy, demanding CRY!

TIP Of course if you really want to stand out from the parenting crowd, why not resist the temptation to boast altogether and go the other way. There is much more fun to be had – and far less pressure – if you underplay your child's achievements:

FRIEND: Look at my boy. He's very bright (*boast, boast*). He's very advanced. Above average, we think (*brag, brag*).

YOU: See my boy? He's as thick as shit. Spectacularly

dim, aren't you, son? As dullards go, he's above average. Don't lick the telly, son, it's only a cookery programme. Oh yes, we can see him being in comfy trousers and slip-on shoes for a very long time.

FRIEND: My son likes to play badminton and chess.

YOU: My son likes to eat mud and flowers.

FRIEND: We've just put our child down for Oxford.

YOU: Really? I've put my boy down for the *Big Issue*.

FRIEND: Does he always pull his doodle so far? It looks very painful.

YOU: Yes. He can strum it like a guitar. Not now, son. There's no music. I knew we should have got a cat.

Accidents

Do happen. That's maybe why you're reading this book.

NOTE It is said that 80 per cent of accidents happen in the home. Which is a shame because we don't get to see them. ***See*** Schadenfreude, Quips, etc.

Adoration (*see also* Gormless staring, Happiness, Photos, etc.)

You may notice that you spend the first few weeks (OK, years) just staring at your baby and smelling her head (it takes all sorts), mesmerised by how cute she is. This is perfectly normal. What is abnormal is carrying her aloft through the town centre on an open-top bus like the FA Cup.

When does adoration stop? *See* Farting.

AdultLine

OK, so we know about the very worthy ChildLine, where children can phone to get help protecting them from horrible adults, but where, you will come to wonder, is 'AdultLine' – where grown-ups can phone someone and get a sympathetic hearing about children and babies who piss *them* off?

'Hello, AdultLine? Thank God you've answered, it's like this . . .

- She won't sleep. I haven't had a decent night's kip for months. She wakes if a chaffinch farts in its sleep in the garden. I'd like her removed from the family home.
- The little bugger giggled at a stranger on the bus today and I haven't had so much as a bloody smile all week. And after I bribed him with a Noddy duvet cover too. It's just not on.
- I've just been woken up at four a.m. on Christmas Day to take delivery of a shoddily made Christmas card. It barely stands up on its own. Rudimentary Christmas scene – a robin sat on a banana. Very little glitter on the product. And after I specifically asked for a cashmere overcoat or an iPod. Can you send social services?

- I'm in my best suit and he's just blown a raspberry at me with a mouthful of pumpkin puree – he thinks it's hilarious, frankly I think it's abuse.

Advice (*see also* Grandparents, Strangers in chip shops, etc.)

Expect plenty. Usually conflicting or just plain bonkers – 'You mustn't let your baby lie on the floor. If you do, evil woodland spirits will enter his body and possess his soul.' Don't be passive in this sea of unsolicited advice/ nonsense. Give it freely to others, and spread the confusion:

- Sheepskin rugs cause galloping back hair in later life.
- You can catch head lice from second-hand teddy bears.
- Don't let her suck her thumb or she'll develop buck-teeth, which are a major cause of academic underachievement.
- Never let a red-haired person kiss the baby before the age of three months or he too will develop thick spongy ginger hair.
- Don't let the dog lick the baby otherwise he'll get worms – and there's nothing worse than a dog with worms.
- Don't let a baby look in the mirror before the age of two unless you want it to develop an attraction for the same sex.
- All babies seen at health centres are secretly graded by the staff and the results passed on to the Government

depending on whether they arrive with the popper points on their clothing done up correctly.

Sadly there don't seem to be any books that give the advice parents need on really important childcare issues such as:

- How to stop the folds in baby's neck growing their own ecosystem.
- Baby flatulence etiquette. Acknowledge or deny?
- Ugly baby etiquette. Ditto.
- Night precautions for baby rolling out of the bed – pillows or trampoline?
- Which clothing patterns best hide bodily secretions – stripes, check or paisley?
- How to avoid suicidal thoughts when negotiating a packed bus with a pram on a day-to-day basis.

Am I ready for fatherhood?

Becoming a dad is an enormous and nerve-racking leap for most men and shouldn't be entered into (if you'll pardon the expression) lightly. If you are in doubt about your paternal capabilities, try this simple test:

1 Your favourite TV programme has begun, maybe Ray Mears' *World of Survival* (am I warm?). You've just settled down with a sandwich and some snacks (mmm, cosy), as Ray's about to show you how to make a fully functioning woman out of some bamboo and banana leaves should you be stranded on a desert island, when

your baby starts crying. Do you a) rush to attend? (10 pts) b) call your partner to attend? (5 pts) c) turn the TV up and feign deafness? (1pt) or d) go to the pub? (0 pts).

2 You get something out of your pocket. You think it's a ten-pound note and offer it to pay a bill, but realise it's a dried-out poo-smeared wet wipe. Do you a) get embarrassed? (0 pts) b) get philosophical? (5 pts) c) act proud? (8 pts) or d) tell them to keep the change? (12 pts).

3 You enjoy dirty looks in restaurants. Yes (5 pts). No (0 pts).

4 You're two hundred miles from home. You discover Miffy, baby's special toy, in the glove box of your car and you know baby can't sleep without it. Do you a) jump back in the car and drive home immediately? (20pts) b) realise there is nothing you can do about the problem, so turn off your phone which is ringing incessantly and lock it in the boot, while comforting yourself that the infant was becoming dependent anyway, you've got to be cruel to be kind, tough love and all that, blah, blah? (5 pts) or c) throw Miffy out the window and deny all knowledge of its existence? (-20 pts).

5 You often think of human excrement in terms of different types of mustard. Yes (10 pts). No (0 pts).

6 You have been carrying around a five-kilo bag of organic compost under one arm for the last month (and it's been seeping toxic substances on to your best shirt) and have

found the whole process an unalloyed joy. In fact you've given it a name. Yes (20 pts). No (-5 pts).

7 You walk into your holiday apartment (Center Parcs – wow, all the fun of a Nottinghamshire rainforest). What do you check for first: a) sharp corners? (5 pts) b) that corks have been put on all objects an idiot could impale himself on, as per your instructions? (20 pts) or c) a minibar? (-10 pts).

Anchors

Aka babies as – figuratively – they're something you can drop overboard to slow you down when you think your life is going too fast.

Arguments

For couples addicted to disagreement but who have run out of things to argue about (the phone bill: 'Look at that, the bill's the same as our phone number, what's the chances of that happening?', suspicious brown marks on the flannel, *EastEnders* or Lobotomy?, etc. – see ***The A–Z of Living Together***), having a baby creates a whole new world of conflict opportunities. Among my favourites are:

- Baby in the bed:

  SHE: Look, every textbook says it's dangerous. You might roll onto him during the night.

  YOU: Well, if I hurt my back, I hurt my back. I'm prepared to take that risk. Now give me some more duvet!

- Nappies: reusable, disposable or (sod the soft furnishings) commando?
- Religion: Catholic, Protestant or Satanist?
- SHE: There's not a lot of point in you offering help if I have to *show* you how to do everything.
  YOU: (*under breath*) I know, that's what I'm relying on.
- Gina Ford, The Baby Whisperer or Jordan?

Asthma (*see also* Obesity)

There is an upsurge of asthma in young children these days, which means blowing out the candles on birthday cakes can become a bit of a marathon. However, it also makes beating them at blow football very easy indeed. Every cloud.

Attitude (*see also* Emotional blackmail, College, Stinginess, etc.)

It is said that having a baby changes the way you look at life. This is true. When the baby is born you will start to see life through the eyes of a much poorer person.

YOU: So the People Carrier (which handles like a cow on Rohypnol) is a few hundred pounds more expensive than the Porsche? Hmm. I've never thought of it like that before. Excuse me while I find a quiet corner to weep.

B

'Baby on board'

Obligatory plastic sign sported by proud parents in the back of their car that explains to potential motorway maniacs that they shouldn't choose your vehicle to crash into as there is a 'baby on board', just in case the half-eaten banana smeared over the window, Postman Pat on repeat on the CD and the stony-faced parents in the front with matching tension eye twitches weren't enough of a clue.

Other vehicle signs you may wish to display to help or confuse other road users:

- Don't follow me . . . I'm driving around aimlessly hoping beyond hope that the little bugger inside will go to sleep.
- Honk if you're fertile.
- If you can read this sign . . . we are looking for a babysitter who can help with homework.
- Baby. I'm bored!
- My other baby's a bastard. (Good luck with this one.) *See also* **Quips**.

Baby carriers aka slings

A fine invention, once you get over the feeling that people are looking at you and imagining you as a hippy – knitting your own sandals and drinking your own pee because it makes you feel better (which is true – once you've drunk your own urine, your day's got to get better, but I digress). All dads should use baby slings; not only do they give you major brownie points with the **yummy mummies** in the children's park (and stop you looking like a sexual deviant in the process), they also give a close approximation to the delights of an advanced-term female pregnancy (without the haemorrhoids, obviously). Try doing up your shoelaces or visiting the toilet with one on for extra pregnancy appreciation. *See also* **Empathy**.

Baby monitors (*see also* Overprotectiveness)

Very useful devices (ignoring baby's privacy issues, of course). When does surveillance go too far? Well, if you've invested in a heart monitor, oscilloscope, movement sensors and a Chip and Pin door entry system, and if your partner is hovering nervously above your baby's head with a mirror suspended over its mouth, checking for globules of moisture every five minutes, you may have gone a tiny bit too far. That said, this is not an area where you want to penny pinch.

SHE: (*with the thing clamped to her ear*) I'm hearing nothing. Is it working properly?

YOU: Of course. I got the most expensive one I could.

SHE: (*alarmed*) No breathing or gurgling? Is he still alive?

YOU: Don't panic.

SHE: Hang on. I'm getting something. Pick up at Cinderella's. Sandra. On the staff account.

YOU: (*incredulous*) The little bugger's operating a minicab business from his cot. You said he was advanced.

SHE: You bastard. I knew you'd buy cheap.

YOU: How dare you. That car boot sale is the finest in the area.

Baby shower

Not a washing aid for babies (although I'm sure they'd love it) but a wonderfully profitable and shamelessly cynical party for mums-to-be to milk their chums for lucrative gifts. Make sure you befriend lots of well-off women a few months before conception. Dads (of course) are overlooked and receive no gifts, but do get a night off from discussing issues like constipation, the correct colour of the nursery for maximum brain development and which of her friends she would most like to be pregnant with at the same time ('wouldn't that be just amazing?'). So not a bad trade-off.

Babysitters

Places to recruit babysitters:

When you have plenty of time:

- Only friends, or friends of friends, from a select inner group of the most trusted of trusted (and only then with impeccable references, you understand. This is our most precious child we're talking about here).

When desperate:

- The pub.
- Next-door's eleven-year-old – so long as it doesn't infringe her Asbo.
- Any passing *Big Issue* seller needing a spare twenty quid and we solemnly promise to be back by nine.

Baby talk

We've all seen people in the park clutching a small bundle and going 'agga wagga lagga lagga oogy woogly woo'. And some of them have children. A few child-rearing manuals (not this one though) stress you shouldn't indulge in such practice but it's perfectly natural – very few babies are born with a firm grasp of English and in a way a baby is like a visitor to your home who comes from a strange and distant land – Kazakhstan, for example. Why not get a Kazakhstani in for a practice run? You wouldn't expect a Kazakhstani to immediately understand the Queen's English, yet you would manage to communicate with him, most of communication being non-verbal anyway – facial expressions; pointing and sounds; farting – and baby talk is really meeting the child half way. They don't speak English, you don't speak baby – you've both got to learn. And if you get good at it, who knows? You may even end up singing scat in a jazz band.

NOTE Baby talk does become addictive, so be careful. You may even find you begin to speak like that to adults.

YOU: (*in exaggerated sing-song tone*) Hello. Peek-a-boo. I can see you.

A rosy-cheeked face appears.

SHE: (*in mock surprise*) There he is . . .

POLICEMAN: If you don't move along, I'm going to nick you for insolence.

SHE: Insolence. That's a big word. Isn't he clever, Dad? Who's a clever boy?

YOU: He's a clever boy.

POLICEMAN: And pinching my cheeks is technically common assault.

Baths

You can't beat bath time. For your child this is a wonderful time too, especially if they have brothers and sisters – splashing about with your siblings in three inches of dilute warm urine with a hint of 'Matey'. Or cosily wrapped up in a towel next to the fire, giggling hysterically as your mum does that tickly drying under the arms trick while blowing raspberries on your belly. But sadly all good things must end. And you're left wondering, Why? Was it your habit of always demanding the end without the taps? Or your insistence on doing your naked impression of a helicopter before you got into the bath? Or was it that your family can afford more hot water now that both you and your sisters are in full-time employment?

Beds (hospital)

One of the perks of a stay in hospital for mum-to-be is that she can finally abandon the pile of **cushions** at home and sleep in those odd multi-adjustable hospital beds that turn your body into various letters of the alphabet at the flick of a switch. Although why anyone wants to have a baby in the shape of the letter 'W', I don't know. Dads who are also staying over for the duration must look on enviously from a wooden chair. As in:

YOU: I got better treatment than this at Gatwick when the French air traffic controllers went on strike.

SHE: Stop moaning. It's not all about *you* any more . . . (see later)

YOU: Bloody national health service. There's people in the hospital morgue more comfortable than me.

SHE: Give it a rest. I'm the one in pain.

YOU: (*under breath*) At least they get their own drawer.

SHE: Oh you do exaggerate. (*see also* **Birthing unit**)

Bets

It's customary during the run-up to the baby's birth for dads or a close friend to organise a fun sweepstake along the lines of: nearest to time of birth, weight, sex, eyes (colour not number, unless you live near one of our nuclear reactors), who it will look like most, bald or in need of a trip to the barbers, that kind of thing.

Bets your partner will not appreciate odds being offered on:

- Number of milliseconds of active labour she endures before demanding the epidural that she vehemently opposed in her birth plan (apparently it's not being *supportive*).
- Number of stitches required to her undercarriage.
- How many hours before it is suggested by Mum or Grandmother that the baby might be 'Advanced'.
- How long before she says, 'I wish my mother would mind her own bloody business.'
- The chances of her ever getting her figure back.
- Number of days before she says, 'Adoption. A terrible decision but mmm, think of the sleep.'
- *Reader add own here.*

Biological clocks

Remember, gentlemen, women's wombs are not made of Teflon. Eggs can stick to them. Hint, hint, or should that be tick, tick?

Birth (The)

There can be few happier and prouder moments in a man's life (except maybe the first time you manage to pee completely over the urinal at school) than watching your partner desperately squatting over a mirror, legs in two different time zones, face the colour of a blueberry muffin, screaming, between gasps of gas and air, 'I'll get you for this, you evil bastard' and thinking: I did that.

Just don't high-five the midwife, she's very busy.

TIP 1 It might be worth having a think about what you want to say when the baby first makes an appearance. Things move pretty fast in the delivery room and you don't want to be caught out with a half-baked verbal offering of 'it's a baby', or the more provocative 'well, what a doddle that was'. (*See also* Contractions)

It must also be remembered that every new parent is notoriously sensitive about their baby and it is very easy to say the wrong thing and cause unintentional hurt. So if you're seeing someone else's newborn child for the first time be careful not to say:

- Good God. Last time I saw something like that it was hanging from a cathedral with water coming out of its mouth.
- Hasn't he got big ears? Is he nocturnal? Does he find his food by echo location?
- Quick, call a priest.
- Ah, what a shame.

TIP 2 If you're a touch on the squeamish side or indeed ever want to enjoy liver and bacon again, do stay away from the business end, and, above all, when things get really painful, do remember to stay out of punching range.

NOTE Don't get fooled by the notion that when you are talking with your partner and her friends about the birth you are actually having a conversation. Remember your role is merely to introduce subjects for *her* to talk about. However, despite the fact that she did 99 per cent of the talking, she'll think that *you* are a great conversationalist. Don't complain, just enjoy the perks – *see* Sex.

Birth plan

Very important document that mums-to-be prepare prior to the baby's arrival. It lists all the major decisions she would like made on her behalf in anticipation that, during childbirth, she will be in such a state of suffering and hormonal confusion that she will be incapable of even saying 'Pain relief? No, I couldn't possibly.' Or 'Any chance of a cheese and pickle sandwich up this end, just to take my mind off things?' Comforting, eh?

Birthing unit

A lot of mums who choose this birth experience for their babies have a dream of a new-age-inspired feng-shui-balanced hospital room (preferably on a ley line), tenderly administered back rubs and ylang-ylang on the oil burner. Unfortunately it is just that, a dream. The reality is a room just the same as any other labour room but with a beanbag thrown in.

Blame

If you are naturally an unsociable individual (e.g., the phone rings on Saturday night and you hope it's *not* for you), having a baby can feel like all your Christmases have come at once. Now you can be as antisocial as you like, as you have a special little someone to blame for all those cancelled trips to dreary meet-ups and dinner parties at tedious friends' houses you're too gutless to say you have nothing in common with except a desperate hollow fear of getting drunk alone.

Bodily changes

Pregnancy creates many changes in a woman's body: stretch marks, bleeding gums, vomiting, piles, diarrhoea, but don't get the wrong idea, it's not all laughs.

Bonding (*see also* Jealousy)

During the early days of baby's arrival it is important for mother and baby to get to know each other and develop that important bond that will last a lifetime (hopefully). At this time it's perfectly natural for dads to get a little envious and resentful:

YOU: (*pacing*) What's going on in that room when she's breastfeeding? Bonding. That'll be it. Freezing me out. Soon there'll be a coup.

I can feel it. I'm outvoted now. Oh God, what a fool I've been. The architect of my own demise. Where's the dog? He's in there with them. The sly bugger! (*see* **Paranoia.**)

'Boo'

The best game in the world. At some point – three months, four months – sometime, placing a sheet over baby and saying, 'Where's baby gone? Where's baby gone?', then removing the sheet and saying, 'Oh, there you are! Boo!', will cause the most beautiful laughter you have ever heard. And you will laugh. And you will do it again and again. Try to stop before the child reaches their mid-twenties, though, or psychological damage may occur.

Books

There are mountains of books on the subject of pregnancy and childbirth. However, if you are undecided on whether to attend the birth, don't read them. The information in these books leaves most men with an expression on their faces that wouldn't be amiss on someone who has received a particularly explorative French kiss from a camel. Alternatively you might prefer to soften yourself up with a few *Alien* films first.

NOTE It may be that the purchase of all these books is merely a quest by your partner to find one which states that several glasses of red wine a day and a few crafty Benson and Hedges are good for foetal development.

Breastfeeding

Natural nursing of your baby should always be encouraged as it increases your baby's immunity from many diseases and (most importantly) Father's immunity from having to get up every two hours for feeding. And it also helps your partner maintain her stupendous new boobs. Although there are drawbacks – *see* **Bonding**.

NOTE Do be careful when commenting on a baby's uncanny resemblance to a family member such as a granddad or brother. Things like this can stick in a mother's mind, leaving her with a very disturbing image when breastfeeding.

Breasts

Or boo-boos as they are actually called (or The Kitchen if you absolutely want to strangle the life out of any notion that one day they may return to anything that approximates to sexual allure). It takes years to get over your fascination with them; and some of us still haven't managed it. (*See also* **Maternity bras, Jealousy, Nipples,** etc.)

Bribes

In order for your house to run smoothly it is important that a clear bribe system is in place for the baby's arrival. Mums and dads may want to implement the following rota system:

Soothing (day) = One back rub

Soothing (night) = Back rub and two breakfasts in bed or half a new pair of jeans

Nappy change (liquid) = One compliment (physical)

Nappy change (solid) = Three compliments (physical – male) or two compliments (intellectual – female)

Bath (with baby) – high scatological danger = A thoughtfully prepared light snack and glass of wine brought to a room of your choice

Bath (baby on own) – Fun = No charge

Nappy bin empty = Small surprise gift value no greater than £2

Rocking to sleep = Snuggle + one compliment or a foot massage (one foot only)

Rocking to sleep (teething) = Foot massage (both feet > ten minutes)

Feeding (breast) = £1 petrol for car

Feeding (bottle) = £0.50 petrol for car or fifteen minutes TV (no interruptions)

Feeding (puree) = £1.50 petrol for car (depending on number of shots on target) or thirty minutes TV (no interruptions)

Morning of baby care = One power nap

Morning of baby care (teething) = Three power naps or a lie-in
Full day of baby care = Sex (no foreplay)
Full day of baby care (teething) = Sex (with foreplay) and a cup of tea afterwards (it's worth a try!)

C

Centre of attention

If, pre-baby, you enjoyed being the centre of attention, having people ask after you, being sought out by friends and family as they entered your home, then you probably shouldn't have had a baby – *see* **'It's not all about you any more'**, etc.

FRIEND: She's lovely.
SHE: I can't stop kissing her. She's so cute.
FRIEND: I know. She's adorable.
YOU: (*entering naked, rubbing your head, distressed*) I've fallen down the stairs. I must have been unconscious for hours. The dogs even took a bite out of me. Didn't anyone see me?

FRIEND: I thought you were just resting. Are you all right?

SHE: He's fine. (*to you*) Be more careful. And don't bleed on the carpet. (*to friend*) Ooh, look, she's trying to have a poo.

FRIEND: Ahhh.

Chastisement (*see also* AdultLine)

It is a sad fact of parenting that children, despite their appearance, aren't cherubs. If for some reason you feel the need to reprimand your child, before you decide to choose corporal punishment and get an invoice some years later for *Dad therapy*, or whatever the blame culture gets round to calling it, you might like to try a more creative method of chastisement:

For teenagers:

- Make them wear a belt or some other trouser-fixing device – to counter the current teenage fashion of wearing your trousers as if you have just had to answer the front door, half way through a dump.
- Turn up at their school wearing a pair of really tight silver spangly shorts. Why not get Mum to dance at a school disco in hot pants and boob tube.
- Insist they take up the tuba or some other unfashionable musical instrument.
- Threaten to tick the box saying you wish to accompany them on their French exchange trip abroad.
- Become a transvestite/policeman.

For all other ages:

- Just give them a really crap haircut.

Checklist for baby's arrival (*see also* Kerching)

There are many things a baby needs that you will have to provide, preferably before its arrival as you'll find it difficult to locate a twenty-four-hour petrol station that sells cribs and sterilising equipment. These include:

MUM:

- Nappies
- Wet wipes
- Abusive names to call your partner during the birth
- Pelvic floor exercise manual (V important)
- Kisses: for baby (mandatory), for partner (optional)
- Well-wishing friends
- Maternity leave plans
- List of new house rules/unreasonable demands
- One strong arm muscle – for carrying baby

DAD:

- Camera
- Cigar
- Selection of sympathetic faces for mother during the birth (very important)
- Earplugs (mandatory)
- Dishevelled appearance (optional)
- Periscope – for baby viewing (*see* Bonding)
- New shed construction manual

- Spare duvet
- Subscription to *Razzle*
- One strong arm muscle – see above

Childhood (stages)

Age:

0–4 months. Boring. Will it ever stop pooing, crying, sleeping and drooling?

4 months–1 year. Fun. If you find having a grinning toothless wriggle worm greet you every morning fun. Which it is, oddly.

1–3. Useless. Too big to pick up, too small to send to the shops for alcohol.

9–14. Useful. Because they can make a cup of coffee without killing themselves.

14–17. Oh dear. If the 'I never asked to be born' drama queen routine doesn't grind your parental dreams into the dust, the house-wrecking parties and pregnancy scares will.

18+. Expensive – *see* **Education**. Makes you wonder what they're eating at university these days, Kentucky Fried Pheasant? Ferrero Rocher sandwiches? Still, there's always that cute university friend who's going through an 'older men are really sexy' phase to look forward to.

Circumcision

If you have a baby boy you may be contemplating whether to have him circumcised. Well, it is cleaner they say, though who uses their foreskin as a waste-paper basket, I don't know. Does it hurt? you may ask. Well, they chop the end of your cock off – you work it out, Sherlock.

TIP If you *do* choose circumcision for your boy, why not purchase a bag of Hula Hoops and store it in the loft. Then when your son brings home a new girlfriend in a few years' time, pop one on the table and say it's his old foreskin. Oh, how they'll laugh.

Cleaning

An excellent byproduct of the third **trimester** of pregnancy is mum-to-be's sudden, strong urge to clean the house from top to bottom – even under the bed, which frankly is just plain weird. This reflex is, presumably, a primal throwback to getting the cave clean for baby's arrival. Dads, all that needs to be said about this is get well out of the way, pour yourself a beer, sit back and let it happen.

Clothes (*see also* Romper suits)

One of the rarely mentioned joys of new parenthood is the simple pleasure gained from dressing your child up in silly outfits every day. Particular favourites are woolly hats that stand up several inches, preferably with huge floppy ears, not to mention oversized slippers with reindeer heads on them. As such, every day becomes fancy-dress day:

YOU: Can you guess what he is today?
SHE: A rabbit?
YOU: They're not ears. They're pulled threads.
SHE: Rumpelstiltskin.
YOU: That was last week.
SHE: A chimney sweep?
YOU: Chimney sweeps wore flat caps. He's wearing a bobble hat.
SHE: One of Santa's little helpers?
YOU: In those dungarees?
SHE: Aha. A lesbian!
YOU: Bingo!

Contractions

How will I know if my contractions have started? According to a lot of women who've been through the experience, rather like getting your fingers slammed repeatedly in a car door, you'll just know.

Wrong things to say during labour (that you only said to take her mind off things, OK?):

- Can you keep the noise down, love, you're putting me off my crossword.
- Try not to strain yourself – we don't want stitches, do we?

- It's funny. You don't *look* in pain.
- Look how blue your face has gone. You could be a Smurf.
- OK, that's your back massage finished; now you do me.
- Is anyone going to have a sandwich? I spent a lot of time making these bloody things, you know.
- D'you think *I'd* be able to cope with the pain?
- 'Can I have some gas and air? Will you turn my TENS machine up? Will someone mop my forehead? Can I have an epidural?' It's all me, me, me today, isn't it, love?

Cravings

For women, along with the development of an acute sense of smell and declarations one minute that you are a wonderful kind-hearted person who is the most fantastic friend anyone could want and the next minute a complete arsehole who's never been there for them whenever they've *really* needed you, you shitbag bastard, cravings are one of mother nature's original pregnancy indicators. Their effects can be quite powerful, although men might be left wondering if this isn't all a big ruse to get them running around like idiots. *See also* **Swinging the lead**, **Is my partner pregnant?**

Crawling

A difficult time for parents occurs around six to nine months as babies develop the habit of not being where you left them. If you get stuck, simply follow the trail of chewed electrical cables, assaulted pets and *Alien*-like drool puddles and you should find your offspring at the end of it. Alternatively, just go straight to the cat litter tray where you'll find baby attempting an impression of a liquorice allsort.

> **TIP Why not get a cat bell collar (search on eBay under 'midget leper accessories')? Or how about one of those extendable dog leads? Combined with a well-buffed laminate floor, that should keep your baby from straying too far.**

Crying

There is a lot of crying with a new baby:

SHE: (*weeping*) Giving birth was *so* overwhelming.

GRANDPARENTS: (*bawling*) My grandchild is so cute and gorgeous.

YOU: (*sobbing*) You paid *how* much for three elephants hanging from a bit of fishing twine?

SHE: It's a hand-crafted, accelerated learning device.

YOU: (*whimpering*) That doesn't make me feel better.

NOTE Having read most of the books on this subject, I can reveal that there are two very important rules you should always follow when attempting to soothe a baby:

1 Always pick it up.

2 Never pick it up.

Clear? Good.

See also Bribes, Nudge (The).

Cushions

All right, we know women love cushions (possibly even more than they love lip balm and cash gifts). The bad news is that during pregnancy her cushion requirements go up several thousand per cent. Most days you will find her sitting Buddha-like on the couch, listing off her daily needs. Things get worse when these cushions find themselves in the bedroom:

Night: The bedroom. Your partner climbs into bed first. All the cushions that have been neatly arranged on her side are tossed over on your side. Some time later you enter the bedroom. For some moments, you survey your side of the bed.

SHE: (*half asleep, looking over her shoulder in your direction*) Are you in bed yet?

YOU: (*staring at a large heap of cushions now blocking your entry to bed*) No, love. Someone's been dry-walling on my side.

SHE: Huh?

YOU: It seems I've got twenty foot of cushion to go before I reach blanket.

SHE: What are you talking about?

YOU: All these bloody cushions. I don't know whether to get into bed or build a croft.

SHE: Well push 'em off. You've got arms.

YOU: (*muttering*) We've got pillows, what do we need cushions for?

She rolls over and covers her head with a pillow.

SHE: What are you wittering on about?

YOU: I said, 'We've got pillows, what do we need cushions for?'

SHE: (*muffled*) I like them. They're part of the coordination.

YOU: You might as well buy a car and stick a motorbike on the top of it.

SHE: That's not a bad idea. Could you get me a motorbike and I'd really like some Afghani hummus as well.

Cutting the cord

One of the unadulterated joys/honours/moments of terror and fainting given to fathers at the birth is the severing of the umbilical cord. If the midwife gives you the chance, take her up on the offer. It's a proud moment, once you get over the mistaken fear that babies are like balloons and a quick snip will send your child flying through the air, deflating loudly. And if the midwife gives you a round of applause, you'll feel as though you've just opened an Asda (but with more photos, less blood, and no points on your loyalty card).

> **WARNING If you are anxious about cutting the cord, which is a delicate procedure, then you might like to leave it to the professionals:**

MIDWIFE: You have a lovely baby boy. Go ahead and cut the cord.

YOU: I'm nervous. I think, erm . . . (*you close your eyes and squeeze*) Did I do it right?

MIDWIFE: But I suppose a girl's just as nice.

D

Dad

the amazing thing about having a baby — that you have created a person who one day will never believe that everything you do, from wonky shelves and misdirected fireworks to wayward coconut-shy balls, is the best in the world. Now that is the miracle of childbirth. Sadly this situation does not last (see Teenagers), but at least this unconditional feeling of admiration does not have to be mutual. So even though you may think at times that you are just a wiper with a wet wipe, you have important [illegible] to fill in your role as father. What it all boils down to is offering encouragement to all your child's

D

Dad

The amazing thing about having a baby is that you have created a person who one day will truly believe that everything you do, from wonky shelves and misdirected fireworks to wayward coconut-shy balls, is the best in the world. Now *that* is the miracle of childbirth. Sadly this situation doesn't last (*see* **Teenagers**), but at least this unconditional feeling of admiration doesn't have to be mutual. So even though you may think at times that you are just a wallet with a wet wipe, you have important duties to fulfil in your role as father. While it is Mum's job to offer blind encouragement to all your child's endeavours, it has been Dad's job throughout history to deliver some withering reality.

Your child removes the recorder from his lips and takes a bow.

SHE: That was wonderful.

YOU: (*under your breath*) Thank God that's over with.

SHE: 'Frère Jacques' on the recorder all by himself. (*She offers a sustained yet solo round of applause. Your son beams with pride.*) Well done, son. What do you think, Dad?

YOU: (*pained*) Honestly? I think he is quite possibly the worst recorder player I have ever had the misfortune to hear.

SHE: Don't listen to him.

YOU: (*ignoring her*) If he weren't my own flesh and blood, I'd set the dog on him.

SHE: Behave.

YOU: Was that a tune or some randomly chosen squawk noises, designed to piss me off?

CHILD: (*whimpering*) It was 'London's Burning'.

SHE: Was it?

DAD: It was awful, that's what it was. Now if I see that recorder at your lips again, I'll shove it up your arse. And I'll probably get a better tune out of it.

SHE: Leave him alone, he's only a child.

YOU: No, he's not. He's twenty-seven.

SHE: Well, he'll always be *my* baby.

NOTE Remember, as a father your role is limited in the early days and weeks after the birth to snack provider, cameraman and emotional punch bag. Try to enjoy it.

Dangers

If as a woman you are pregnant while reading this (I probably didn't need to say the 'as a woman' bit) then you may be forgiven for thinking that there are so many possible ways to accidentally harm your unborn foetus that it is probably best if you hide away in a hermetically sealed room and have your partner pass folic acid sandwiches to you under the door. It is also possible that your partner, far from being the passive slob of old, is now taking a far greater interest in what you are doing during your pregnancy than he has ever done before and thinks that when he's not looking you are swigging vitamin A milkshakes, gorging yourself on liver pâté and goat's cheese pizzas while making pretty little finger paintings using a palette of unpasteurised cat poo. This may be true but hey, when you're the size and shape of an overstuffed Teletubby and the only thing to look forward to in your day is a few minutes rubbing the deep red marks on your hips left by the elastic of your oh-so-attractive maternity trousers, you've got to get your kicks from somewhere.

Difficult birth

Apparently this means pain, complications, touch and go whether mother or child will pull through unscathed. It does not mean the hospital vending machine only had wine gums and vegetable cup-a-soup left and the nearest pub was so far away it was bloody hard to get there and back *and* down a swift half between her contractions. Apparently.

Dilation

Ten centimetres. That's the size of an arm. Do we really *need* to be told?

Disappointment

When you finally manage to get your first wide gummy smile from baby and then realise the only thing that triggered it was trapped gas. But hey, they all count. Soon babies learn that gas = smile and for men this continues well into adulthood.

Drinking (during pregnancy)

OK, your partner has given up alcohol for the duration of the pregnancy, so if *you* think you're going to get away with copious drinking while she abstains, think again. Every drop, every molecule, every boozy smile, every beery kiss will be counted for use as ammunition later, when frankly you've forgotten about it and moved on.

SHE: Having another, are we?

YOU: It's only shandy.

SHE: That's the third.

YOU: I've had one.

SHE: Three.

YOU: When?

SHE: That one. One yesterday. One in the Snooty Fox a week last Tuesday. There, three. And don't think I've forgotten that chocolate liqueur I saw you sneakily neck at Gran's in March.

YOU: Bloody hell. It's like living with a regiment of the Salvation Army

NOTE If you've ever woken up after a large night out and wondered where all those odd bruises on your legs and body came from, then now you know.

YOU: (*perplexed*) Where have all these bruises come from? I've only been to the pub. Did I get a cab home or was I dragged naked? Did four dwarves kick the crap out of me?

SHE: I did them. No one drinks when I can't.

Drool

According to strange people who take an interest in these things, we produce sixty-six gallons (two hundred and ninety-seven litres) of saliva in our lifetimes. As a new parent eyeing your soggy furniture, and your once beautifully kept clothes, the shoulders of which are fast becoming a biohazard, you will come to think that most of it is produced in the first year. Indeed, babies produce as much saliva as a St Bernard dog chewing an Opal Fruit downwind from a sausage sizzle.

Possible uses for baby drool:

- Wallpaper paste
- Squeaky door repair fluid
- Emergency hair gel
- Vegan egg white replacement
- Clearing stragglers from a party:

YOU: (*handing over a jam jar*) This is my son's drool. Would you like to take some home with you? We've got plenty.

Drugs

There are many narcotics available to assist mothers with the birth – gas and air, pethidine, paracetamol, brandy and coke. For fathers, however, there are fewer options available (especially if you foolishly swigged the emergency supply of

Night Nurse on New Year's Eve). Fortunately, I can make a suggestion. Why not try inflating the birthing pool without using the supplied foot pump? Half an hour blowing that up using just your lungs and I guarantee you'll be up there with your partner in la-la land. And not a bad place to have a lie-down and a nice soak afterwards.

Dummies

Is the baby using a dummy? Yes. He's in a sleeping bag outside Mothercare waiting for the sales. Although we prefer the term 'Daddy'.

E

Education

The schooling of your child is very important, although it has been estimated (by gloating singles, no doubt) that it costs over one hundred thousand pounds to put a child through school and university. Which may inspire some parents to secretly hope that their little one turns out to be a bit of a duffer.

YOU:	How's he doing, miss?
TEACHER:	It's not been a good term. He's a willing and popular boy but I can't deny he's struggling.
YOU:	In what way?

TEACHER: Well, last week we discovered him talking to the wax crayons and the week before that we found him standing in the playground trying to eat the wind. So I'm afraid we don't think he's ready for GCSEs just yet.

YOU: (*under your breath*) *Yes!*

TIP In order to afford your child's education you may have to apply a few economies to his upbringing. For example, why not buy your child's toys from the pet shop? Kitten balls and budgie mirrors make ideal Christmas gifts. Alternatively you could consider selling one of your kidneys on the Internet. (NB: selling one of *their* kidneys is considered socially unacceptable, for some reason) *See also* Stinginess.

Emotional blackmail

New mums know it can be much easier to get your own way once you have an incredibly cute third person toddling around the home. The important phrase here is *your child*. Do be sure to use it as often as possible, to gain maximum leverage, as in:

- Loosening up the house finances – Well, if it's too much money, I can always dose *your child* on Calpol and take him on the streets with a little cardboard notice until we get enough money to buy *your child* a proper pram.
- Shopping trip avoidance – If you're happy for me to

drive *your child* in heavy traffic when I'm delirious with exhaustion after only ten minutes' sleep, then yes, I can go to the shops.

- New clothes demand – I've cut the feet out of his romper suit, that should give him a few more days' wear, so if you're happy that they've started calling *your child* Huckleberry Finn at the health centre, that's fine.
- Parkland walk request – I suppose I'll just have to have these golden memories (that you won't get back, you know) of *your child* drooling on some ducks' heads all to myself. Anyway, there's always lots of single men lurking in the park for me and *your child* to talk to. (*See also* **Kerching**, etc.)

Emotions

The trouble with having a baby is that for some reason everything around you suddenly becomes so annoyingly poignant.

SHE: Pass me the broccoli.

YOU: Broccoli. So fragile. Just like our child.

SHE: (*tasting*) Oh, it's cold. I'll put it in the microwave.

YOU: I hope our child is never cold. And lost, on a hillside. Needing his dad. (*sniffle*) Excuse me. I've got to go and give him a hug.

SHE: You're not right, you. (*See also* **Hormones**)

Endorphins

Forget heroin, crack or even Rice Krispie chocolate crackles. Endorphins are the 'happy hormone', naturally produced by the female body. And probably the only thing standing between you and certain painful death during your partner's many difficult stages of pregnancy and childbirth.

Euphemisms

It's worth keeping a few informal names handy for those *private* areas. Choose from the following:

BOY: Winkle, Pinky, Doodle, Pee Pee, Prince Edward.
GIRL: Auntie Mary, Front Bottom, Flat Willy, Elizabeth (Regina), George (Bush: this one works on a couple of levels).

You should also encourage the use of those childhood words in adult life – it might stop men wanting to speed around in flash cars.

FEMALE: Nice sports car.
YOU: (*smiling broadly*) Thank you.
FEMALE: But then it *is* just an extension of your winkle.
YOU: (*deflated*) I don't feel like driving it now. That was really mean of you.
FEMALE: I know. I'm such a front bottom.

Exaggeration

We all inflate the difficulties of new parenting. It's part of the fun at a time when we need all the appreciation and love (but mostly appreciation) we can get. Why say the baby was born in twenty minutes when you can say it took thirty hours, you're lucky to be alive and they had to pull the baby out with a tractor? Why say there was only your bloke, a donkey and a couple of mangy sheep at the birth when you can say three men in crowns turned up with fabulous gifts?

YOU: We couldn't get anywhere to stay, you know. And with her ready to drop an' all.

FRIEND: It sounds a nightmare.

YOU: And some. Eventually they gave us some smelly old stable. I said, you're having a laugh, aren't yer?

FRIEND: No birthing pool, hot towels, whale music?

YOU: Nowt. And the only light was from a star, shining through a gap in't roof. The missus was livid.

FRIEND: I'll bet.

YOU: It was that bad, she reckons someone'll write a book about it one day.

FRIEND: It must've been bad. So what's your boy up to?

YOU: Carpenter now.

FRIEND: It's useful to have a trade to fall back on.

YOU: Drink?

FRIEND: What you got?

YOU: Wine. The lad made it out of water.

FRIEND: He's clever.

YOU: Yes. (*whispering conspiratorially*) Above average, even 'special' they say (that'll do, Jeff).

TIP If your partner is one of those people who lives by the adage 'never let the facts get in the way of a good story' (don't they all?), you may well witness the slow dawn of a legend as she regales the hordes of friends, relatives and people in bus queues (believe me, she won't be fussy) who now gather to drink up the gory details of her labour and birth. The labour will grow from three hours to twelve, to twenty, then to days. The pain will rise from a niggly ache to grievous bodily harm. At this point you will begin to question your own memory of events and if in fact you were even at this epic life event. What you mustn't do is poo-poo her claims. Let her enjoy herself. If you don't, you run the risk of her storing up the slight against her good name, in public too – oh dear (logged in the same place she's keeping all those times you showed her up at parties). And by agreeing with her now you can win some brownie points to redeem against nocturnal baby duties later, or at least an uninterrupted half an hour of Ray Mears with the headphones on. It's worth a try.

NOTE It goes without saying that no one cares how harrowing the birth was for *you*, so shush about the nightmare you had parking, the lack of a bed for you, the huffing and puffing in your ear, the fingernail bruises on your arm, which really hurt actually, the measly packet of wine gums for breakfast, the unfinished Sudoku, *and* let's not forget what all this new baby stuff bloody cost you. (*See* 'IT'S NOT ALL ABOUT YOU ANY MORE'.) Still, only twenty years to go and it'll be just like the old times again, but with less hair obviously.

Excuses

Dads: you are bound to make a few parenting errors in the first few months. Off-the-peg excuses you may need before you eventually get into your stride:

- Expensive baby shoe missing – Hey look, we found a shoe!
- Unchanged nappy – I'm just too much of a romantic. I prefer it when we do things *together*.
- Eyeing up other mums at the NCT meet-up – My God. You've got your figure back much more quickly than any of those other women.
- Bringing baby home crying, soaking wet, covered in pondweed – 'I'm sorry, darling, I was just writing you this love letter when I heard a splash. It's a bit wet, but you can still make out all the kisses at the bottom. (Good luck with this one.)

- Caught watching football instead of *Noddy Goes to Toytown* – I was working on the principle of aeroplane emergencies where they say it's very important to put your *own* oxygen mask on first.

Mums: *see* **Emotional blackmail**.

Extended babysitting

Or adoption as some people insist on calling it.

F

Farting

Prepare to be shocked. You will be amazed by the volume, the smelliness and the regularity. And yet it is not mentioned in any child-rearing book.

Dealing with your child's wind is just about tolerable during daylight hours, but do be careful if you allow baby into your bed at night.

YOU:	Oh, no. He's guffed again. He's unbelievable.
SHE:	It means he's comfortable in our company.
YOU:	True, although if *I* let off like that you'd have me sleeping in the car. (*pause*) This one's really

bad. It's like there's been an explosion in a pickled egg factory . . .

SHE: Hey, don't waft. He's your child too.

YOU: Well, you're feeding him the bum fuel. What's he noshing on these days, pureed Guinness and lentils?

SHE: Are you sure that's one of his and not you?

YOU: Me? If I could fart like that, I'd have my own show on Bravo. I reckon you're using him as a decoy to let some of your own gas out.

SHE: How *dare* you.

YOU: In fact, now I think of it, there was a hint of Pinot Grigio in that last one. Yes, definitely Pinot Grigio. 'Crisp and fresh with a zesty acidity.' I'm on to you. You're a ventriloquist guffer, that's what you are.

SHE: (*guiltily turning over*) Oh you do exaggerate.

(*See also* Smells not even a mother could love.)

NOTE Cupcaking – if you thought you'd left behind at school the practice of lifting a handful of farty air into the nose of an innocent victim, then having a baby and the unlimited amount of whiffy guff it produces will change your mind. Being 'hilariously' cupcaked by mum is often a feature of those early months. As they say, it's good to share. *See also* Immaturity.

Father blues

A medically overlooked male reaction to childbirth experienced by new dads. Symptoms include looking out of the window dewy-eyed as you realise it's going to be a long time before you do anything on the spur of the moment ('Let's go to Paris for lunch!') or read a book all the way through that's not made out of cloth.

Fathers Day (see also Mother's Day)

The day your child will show you how much they love you by buying you a 'best dad in the world' mug with your own money.

NOTE Why not petition the Government to officially rename the other three hundred and sixty-three days *Children's Day*. These days would be celebrated with hugs, cash gifts, free meals and transport. That way parents might just get a glimmer of appreciation.

First words

Often preceded by a battle between Mum and Dad as to who gets their name uttered first. Only one thing is certain, it won't be 'Thank you'.

TIP 1 If having your name said first is important to you, why not simply change your name by deed poll to

Ackawaggaduckadacacopuchu to give yourself a fighting chance?

TIP 2 If you are feeling left out when discussing child milestones with other mums, i.e., everyone else's baby is crawling, sitting up, sleeping through the night and borrowing their copy of *Puzzler* while yours is still cross-eyed and trying to eat his own feet, why not quietly lie about your child's age? Shaving a few months off here and there (a year's good if you can get away with it) can make all the difference to those playgroup discussions.

WOMAN: Really, talking at three months?

YOU: Yes, isn't it good, although he's not interested in playing Boggle with us any more.

WOMAN: He's big for three months.

YOU: Tell me about it. Every time the missus puts a hat on him, her eyes water at the memory.

Firsts

There are many firsts that are important to new parents: first breath, first look, first trip out (after the birth – planned ahead so you can iron out any expressions of excessive pride, bewilderment and fear from your face), first smile, tooth, bottle, full night's sleep, giggle, false giggle, poo without a nappy on (not a good day), Christmas, solid meal, finished meal, word, swear word, lie, complaint, answer back, apology, trip to casualty with a button up the nose, balloon, lost balloon, delivery of cup of tea in bed (tepid, made from water out the tap, nine sugars, brought in with such concentration on the face – with their tongue sticking out because they need more room in their head to think about it, but you're overjoyed), pair of long trousers, pet, pet death (what do you mean, you were changing the batteries? Hamsters don't have batteries), bike, broken tooth, sleepover, fist fight, sports day, bullying incident, Monopoly tantrum, runaway threat, arson incident, girlfriend, boyfriend, period, request not to hold hands in public any more, Eggnog-induced chunder, phone call in the middle of the night from the police, Asbo, best friend fall-out, suspicious bed stains, offer to wash own sheets and pyjamas from now on, toxic overuse of Lynx body spray, spot, love bite, shave, utterance of the phrase 'I never asked to be born', broken loan agreement, unauthorised use of your credit card, sleepover at opposite-sex house, pregnancy scare, broken heart, demand to go to an all-night rock festival – nine of you in a two-man tent? – cosy, suspicious pupil dilation, well-argued victory over you in a political debate, driving lesson, job interview, move out, moment of eerie peace as you wonder what the hell you're going to do now. Move back in. Oops, spoke too soon.

Five phases of babyhood

1 Liquids in. Liquids out.
2 Liquids in. Liquids and gas out.
3 Liquids in. Liquids, gas and smiles out.
4 Liquids in. Liquids, gas, solids, grunts and smiles out.

5 Liquids and solids in. Liquids, gas, solids, grunts, smiles and teeth out.

Congratulations. You have made it past stage one.

Fertility (male)

Conceiving a child stirs up many emotions, not least relief that those nylon underpants you wore during your youth, and the associated static electricity they produced, haven't caused any long-term damage. After all, it can't be very healthy for your precious spermatozoa if your scrotum is being tasered twice a day by man-made fabrics. (Female: *see* Biological clocks)

Flash forwards

The opposite of flashbacks. These often arrive in your head at odd moments as you ponder what joys/terrors the future might hold for you as a parent. E.g., you're:

- Dad: Sat in a Chuckle Brothers concert. Even worse, you're enjoying it.
- Mum: Looking in a careers shop window with your (now) out-of-date skills, contemplating the minimum-wage cleaning job or the nightshift petrol station attendant position.
- Dad: Waiting outside a suburban house at nine o'clock in your car while a teenage party rages inside, wondering if anyone cares that you're missing Ray Mears' *World of Survival*.

- Mum: Hearing 'Just sign it, Mum. It's not that we want to get rid of you, we just want to make sure you get looked after properly, by professionals.'
- Both: Eating dog-food sandwiches alone in a bedsit in Rhyl.

Forgetfulness

Remember when you could leave your house in a few seconds:

YOU: Party at Alan's? Strippers? Finger food? Vol au vents? Badly spelled tattoos? Hold that bra strap, I'll be there in ten minutes.
A quick check of keys, phone, 'Unleash the Beast' underpants, socks, wallet, face set to 'Hello ladies'. And you were away.

This will not happen any more.

YOU: (*Sunday morning*) Ready?
SHE: Yes.
YOU: OK, let's go. Now I've looked at the map and we should have plenty of time to get to IKEA. Hmm, Sunday walking round IKEA, I'm living the dream.
SHE: (*ignoring you*) I'll just grab his hat.
YOU: OK.
SHE: And an extra blanket.

YOU: Got it all here. (*you pat a bulging bag*)

SHE: Have you seen his mittens?

YOU: It's not cold out.

SHE: What's the temperature?

YOU: Warm.

SHE: Warm for you. He's a baby.

YOU: Really? I wondered about the drool and why he never seemed to go out to work.

SHE: No need for sarcasm. Got the car seat?

YOU: Yes.

SHE: Spare nappies.

YOU: Yes.

SHE: What about Buzzy?

YOU: Buzzy? What the bloody hell is that?

SHE: *Language*. He can hear, you know. Buzzy. It's his little friend. The soft toy from Gran. It's a cuddly bee.

YOU: I'm one step ahead of you. It's in the bag.

SHE: Stroller or sling?

YOU: Stroller. It's already in the boot.

SHE: But the sling's so much easier.

YOU: OK, sling.

SHE: Are you sure?

YOU: No. Of course not. Whatever you want.

SHE: Are there stairs or escalators?

YOU: I don't know. I didn't manage to see the blueprints.

SHE: I'll take the sling.

YOU: I like your decisiveness. The sling it is. Let's go.

SHE: Oh, hang on; do you think he's hungry?

YOU: He looks fine.

SHE: I'll just give him a boob. It'll save him whingeing in the car.

YOU: Love. The time.

SHE: Oh dear. Nappy change.

YOU: I give up.

SHE: It'll take two seconds.

YOU: I'll get the wet wipes.

SHE: He'll be fine.

YOU: Are you sure?

SHE: (*snaps*) Yes.

YOU: But what if he gets a chapped bottom?

SHE: (*spelling it out as if talking to an orang-utan*) He'll – be – fine.

YOU: (*backing off*) OK.

SHE: Your trouble is you fuss too much.

NOTE It is preordained that you always forget something on a journey out with mother and baby, usually your sense of humour.

Friends

These can be divided into two groups: those with children and those wasting their lives living a vacuous consumerist existence – *see* **Lucky bastards**.

NOTE The simple truth is by having a baby you will lose friends, and gain some – new friends, better friends, babysitting friends, friends who understand that the dried pumpkin in your hair is an occupational hazard not a lifestyle choice. *See also* Visitors.

G

Gas and air

Three cheers for Mr Entonox! *See also* **Drugs**.

Gears

You will notice your baby has only four states early on – silent, loud, ear-wax-meltingly loud and a noise that calls upon God to release this poor individual from his earthly torment, or at least help me bring up this burp.

Getting baby to sleep

There are few tragedies worse in a parent's life than taking several hours to put your baby down – lullabies, rocking, driving round the M25, offering your soul to the god of sleep for just half an hour of REM please, before finally against the odds succeeding in inducing the fragile miracle of sleep, and as you lift baby gently, desperately towards some soundproof box with barely concealed relief and joy, you accidentally tread on a baby synthesiser. Suddenly lights start flashing and the room fills with an ear-splitting electronic bloody tango. The eyes open. The mouth follows. The noise erupts and all hope of half an hour with another grown-up is extinguished.

> **NOTE** This error is very similar to 'The Drop', whereby the last couple of inches to the mattress in the cot is misjudged when putting baby down and a moment of free fall occurs. Thus in an instant all your hours of soothing are undone. All I can say is, believe me, I feel your pain. *See also* Zzzzz.

Getting your own way . . . (men)

When confronted with a situation involving baby where you and your partner hold strongly opposing beliefs, give your partner her own way. Due to innate contrariness (attributed to your partner's exposure to oestrogen in the womb apparently), she will then decide she doesn't want her own way and so de facto you get what you want. Everyone's a winner. Unfortunately now I have told you this, I must kill you.

Women: Just ask for whatever you want with that same homicidal twinkle that was in your eye during labour. Failing that, *see* **Emotional blackmail**.

Grandparents

If you are estranged from your parents then you must make sure you get back on good terms before the baby arrives, otherwise their unpaid babysitting skills and easily tweaked financial assistance will go unused and that is criminal. Grandparents are great too for a bit of silent judging on a bank holiday weekend. *See also* **Advice, Love (unconditional.)**

Guilt (mother's)

An insidious feeling experienced by women that they are not doing the 'right thing' for their baby – 'Is she sleeping enough? Is he eating enough? Am I showing her enough love? Will that time I didn't hear him crying for three and a half seconds lead to expensive therapy bills later in life?' Interestingly, fathers may notice there is no such thing as Wife's Guilt, as you set out once more into the pouring rain for more nappies from the corner shop, checking on the way to see if you've got enough coppers for a Ginsters

Cornish pasty for your Sunday dinner, as you slowly wither and die from sexual frustration and a lack of basic human kindness in your shed with a bottle of brandy in one hand and your 'old chap' in the other. Let it go, Jeff.

H

Hairdryers

Gently wafted on a baby's bottom, a hairdryer is a practical and fun way to dry all those folds and crevices. Don't do it too much though, or it may give them sexual problems later on in life, or at the very least a strong urge to 'moon' people from fast cars. *See* **Tory MPs**.

Health centres

Where babies are taken for check-ups, inoculations, weighing, to collect and pass on the latest infections doing the rounds, and to be covertly graded by other mums on a sliding scale from Cherub to Extra-terrestrial. *See also* **'Best in Show' rosettes, Illnesses**, etc.

Holding the baby

If you have fears about holding your baby properly (it is difficult early on – their heads and necks are very floppy and their posture resembles that of Pope John Paul II during his later years), why not get a seamstress friend to run you up a couple of Velcro suits – one for you and one for the baby. Then whenever you want to take him out, you can just stick him on you – hey presto! No more storage problems in the local pub for the pram – bring him along, stick him on the flock wallpaper and make your way to the bar.

Honesty

Although your partner may say that above anything else she values honesty in the relationship, you must be careful not to be *too* honest. Women are notoriously fickle at this time – *see* **Hormones**. For example, avoid situations such as:

SHE: And that's why I think we should buy the little-wheeled buggy, not the big-wheeled one. What do you think?

YOU: I'm sorry, love, I wasn't listening. I was distracted by that woman's knockers over there.

SHE: (*tearful*) Where've you been? I've been shouting for ages. I had to bring all the shopping in on my own.

YOU: I know, I heard you. I was keeping quiet in the back.

SHE: Do these jeans make me look fat?

YOU: No. I think it's all the ice cream you've been eating that's doing that for you. Hey, that wasn't a slap – that was a punch.

REMEMBER Women are human and value honesty only when it's ruthlessly applied to dissecting the faults of people they don't like (which hopefully doesn't include you).

NOTE Of course, there has always been a distinction between being honest with your partner and with your children. Some say that it is wrong to tell children lies *See also* Advice, Knowledge, Dad, etc. These people are dimwits and should not be listened to. Of *course* you should lie to children. They're actually the best people to lie to. For a start if they catch you out they are not going to hit you. Well, not very hard. Children appreciate very early on that lying is fun and lucrative especially if attached to the right kind of crime (*see* Naughtiness). And what parent is going to be so cruel as to say to their child:

- Son, I saw you in the school play today and have to say that was quite possibly the shabbiest characterisation of a shepherd I've ever seen in my life. I was so embarrassed I was tempted to throw my complimentary mince pie at you. And where does it say in the Bible: 'Lo, Jesus will be met by three waving, gormless bloody idiots with cotton wool on their faces'? Not in my Bible, matey boy.
- Son, your mum and I have had a meeting and think it's best if you don't bring home any more Rice Krispie chocolate crackles from domestic science classes. Mr Kipling you are not. In fact, the last lot you brought home were so poorly made, when I handed them out to guests, I had to tell everyone you were partially sighted.
- CHILD: Where's Fido, Daddy?
  YOU: Ah, yes. Well, we couldn't really afford him any more so we've had him gassed by the vet. He's in a wheelie bin around the back if you want to say goodbye to him.
- CHILD: Does Granny want one of my flapjacks?
  YOU: No, darling, we've only just got her back on solids thanks to your cooking.
- CHILD: Is the gerbil hibernating?
  YOU: No, son, your mum and I got drunk and used him in a sex game. He's probably just having a breather. And if you've touched him, wash your hands.

Hormones – *see also* Endorphins

There is a good chance that during your partner's pregnancy you will come to believe that overnight you have developed remarkable storytelling skills and that, by the mere retelling of a trip to Aldi for cheap Cava, you can reduce her to tears of pathos. Before booking your world tour, bear in mind this is merely a temporary phenomenon: there are currently more hormones pumping through your partner's system than you'd find in an average Tour de France cyclist (allegedly). Luckily men don't have any.

Hospitals – *see* Birthing unit, etc.

House plants

If yours resemble pot pourri or indeed you can only be trusted with the plastic variety, then you might want to rethink the idea of having a baby.

Hygiene

It is very important to keep certain baby items sterile – bottle teat, teething ring, spoon, etc. This means more than just giving them a bit of a blow or a lick and a wipe on your cardigan, apparently.

I

Illnesses – *see also* Health centres

CAUTION Now you have had a baby, you are living with a human Petri dish that will collect, incubate, ferment and grow to toxic levels every bacteria and virus known to medical science (but then I suppose licking all the other children's toys in the playgroup while your back is turned will do that). One day baby will innocently sneeze on you, you'll laugh, wipe your face and the next morning wake up, eyes streaming and coughing like a Labrador on a choker lead. This cycle of infection will increase until you expire prematurely or the child leaves home, whichever is the sooner.

Inoculations

Very important injections to guard baby from developing life-diminishing problems later in life. Although there is as yet no medical protection against baldness, fat ankles or having a tedious personality, which is a shame. *See also* **K vitamin**.

Involuntary bodily functions

I'm sorry to break it to you but some (all right most) women accidentally (so they say) 'visit the bathroom' during childbirth. Worth mentioning in case your partner was contemplating having a curry to bring the baby on, or if you were thinking of wearing expensive loafers for the birth. *See* **Pelvic floor exercises**.

> **NOTE** The days when it was common practice for a woman to receive an enema and have her privates shaved in preparation for childbirth are long gone (killjoys). Now instead of cutting down a piece of garden hose and sharpening your cut-throat razor, you'll have to content yourself with watching daytime TV and fending off several hundred 'Has she had it yet?' texts and phone calls.

Is my partner pregnant?

The early stages of pregnancy are a difficult time, especially if you have had trouble conceiving up to this point.

There are, of course, very accurate testing kits available from the chemist, but as a back-up why not try this handy quiz:

- She's just eaten chocolate eclair and chips, twice. (15 pts)
- She can't remember where her keys are, her own phone number or why she let your rancid carcass near her in the first place. (12 pts)
- Her morning flatulence doesn't seem to have any impact on her (expanding) Buddha belly. (20 pts)
- She's staring like a hypnotised chicken at any miniature clothing she sees in shop windows. (15 pts)
- Her periods have become barely commas. (10 pts)
- She's quietly locked away the nipple clamps. (25 pts)
- She thinks eighty quid for a raffia 'Moses' basket (made by inmates of a Chinese insane asylum) is really quite reasonable. (15 pts)
- She's just punched a nun. (25 pts)

'IT'S NOT ALL ABOUT YOU ANY MORE'

The universal truth that all fathers must face up to eventually. Often pointed out at maximum volume across the bedroom at three o'clock in the morning after you innocuously ask if, as she's up with the baby anyway, she would mind making you a cheese and pickle sandwich.
See also **'Why do I have to do EVERYTHING around here?'**, etc.

J

Jacuzzis

If you suspect you might be pregnant then you are specifically warned to keep out of these, although if you're one of our modern suburban swingers this advice might be a case of shutting the stable door after the horse has bolted.

Jealousy

As a dad, it is normal to feel slightly resentful about your new 'glorified waiter' role during those first few days back at home with your baby, as you stand, meerkat-like, trying to get a better view, before plodding forlornly away from the cosy vision that is your newborn child snuggling up to Mum:

SHE: (*holding baby close to her warm bosom*) We won't be taking visitors for a while. Just close the door on the way out.

YOU: Does that mean me too?

SHE: Yes. We're very tired. Just leave some nibbles, maybe a glass of milk and a few chilled grapes outside the door, there's a love. I'll text you if *we* need anything.

YOU: (*walking away, head bowed*) OK. I'll be in the kennel if you need me. Don't worry about me, I've got a pot noodle and a new *Razzle* that should get me through the night. (*hearing nothing*) I said I've got a pot noodle and a . . .

SHE: (*angrily*) Shhh. He's sleeping. You are so selfish these days.

Does she love the baby more than she loves me?

If you suspect you are feeling jealous, surreptitiously try one of these simple tests on your partner and observe her reaction:

- After a particularly big night out, keep her awake all night as you restlessly complain of overindulgence. As she soothes you, vomit on her breasts.

- One morning, in bed, wake her with an affectionate smile and a lime-green crust of mucus moving rhythmically with each breath in and out of your nose. Perhaps reach forward and kiss her.
- During a dinner party sidle up to your partner and whisper gently into her ear that you think you'd better leave as you've just soiled yourself in the kitchen.

If after any of these scenarios you have received less than fulsome support and understanding, then sadly, there's your answer.

See also **Bonding, 'IT'S NOT ALL ABOUT YOU ANY MORE', Guilt (Mother's)**, etc.

Joy of sex

Unfortunately, since the birth, with the arrival of your under-eye bags and worry-induced hair loss, and her droopy boobs and saggy arse, you may need to develop a sex life no longer based on mutual attraction. Not to be confused with **Misery of sex**.

TIP Be careful if you have sex in the dark during this time (the light might wake the little one). There are many hazards associated with this, not least when you think you've taken her blouse off and find you've changed the duvet cover.

YOU: Could we have a bit of light please, love?

SHE: I'm shy.

YOU: You may well be shy, but I don't possess sonar equipment. I've been orally pleasuring your 'Tickle me Elmo' for half an hour, the condom you gave me was an Alka-Seltzer and the cat thinks I've just taken its temperature.

SHE: Oh, you do exaggerate.

K

Kerching!

Or, to put it another way, 'I'm shopping for two now'. If you thought pregnancy, labour and a little bundle of neediness that requires feeding every two hours might slow the haemorrhaging of your wallet, you are sadly mistaken. And with the invention of the Internet (oh dear!), there is no shortage of overpriced tat – *sorry* – baby essentials available to purchase twenty-four hours a day:

- 101 whale songs to calm your baby
- Hand-crafted baby jewellery aka Baby Bling
- The Endangered Cuddly Animal Collection
- Ethnically crafted organic teething ring

- Silk christening gown and matching hand-stitched jodhpurs (one day use only)

See also **Cynicism**, **Stinginess**, etc.

Knitting

Hurrah for grannies and nanas. There is nothing these indispensable family members can't knock up with a bit of old woollen thread and some pointy metal chopsticks – booties, balaclavas, even a discreet spare toilet roll cover (with a little smiley face crocheted on, suggesting he can't wait to help perform the service of wiping your bottom). However, be careful with requests. Once started it seems they don't stop.

Knitted items your child will not thank you for when s/he grows up (especially if there is photographic evidence):

- Swimming trunks or bikini
- Football kit, including boots
- Fairy wings
- Elvis Presley Vegas-era jumpsuit (I've seen them, they *exist*!)
- Any superhero outfit, with crocheted cloak

Knowledge

Don't worry if you find there is something you don't know when it comes to bringing up your child. Grandparents know everything about babies and will be more than happy to tell you what you are doing wrong, often without even being asked, bless them. Failing that, you'll find lots of strangers in shops and in the street delighted to offer unbidden advice and/or a full critique of your child-rearing skills to date. This is because people who have had children view all babies as citizens of the world. Of course, knowing this won't stop you wanting to stab them in the eye with a teething rusk. *See also* **Advice**.

K vitamin

Often the very first thing that happens to a newborn is a painful jab of this vitamin in the foot. An apt welcome to the world, which leaves them in no doubt that it's all downhill from here, baby.

L

Labour

Generally comes in three stages:

For Mum

1 Excruciating pain
2 More excruciating pain
3 The excruciating pain continues

For Dad

1 Gentle low-level concern
2 Slight anxiety

3 Gormless support giving way to mild relief (light weeping optional)

Labour lag

A little-known effect whereby parents are fooled into thinking that the delightful docile newborn they held in their arms in the delivery room will be the same baby they will be holding in three days' time. 'Aren't we lucky?' they coo. 'So quiet, sleeps the sleep of the just.' Wrong. Often junior is just having a breather while s/he recovers from the exertion of birth. Once strength is regained it will, dear parents, reveal its true nature. How? With a cry. And I mean a CRY!! A cry you thought only members of the Spanish Inquisition and people forced to watch reruns of *EastEnders* for ever have heard. You have been warned. *See* **Earplugs**, etc.

Last days of freedom

Even more important than a stag night or hen party should be an evening to mark, nay, rejoice/mourn* the end of your carefree days before that little life-magnet lands in your lap.

This evening should cover as many things as possible that you won't be enjoying over the following several weeks/months/years:

1 Gin and tonics. Several and large. Not mum, though (boo hoo).

2 Dinner – Somewhere quiet and densely packed in (no room for prams).

3 Food – Anything off the menu that requires both hands to eat.
4 Movie – 18 cert MINIMUM, preferably something you can't get on DVD or the cartoon channel.
5 Nightclub – Loud. Don't book a cab. You're not sure when you're coming home.
6 Home – Giddy ride back to sex/a book*, yes a whole book made of real paper, damn it, followed by a long, uninterrupted sleep, awaking late afternoon the next day. Bliss.

*Delete as applicable

Leakage

If your partner is breastfeeding, you may notice that you are now sleeping with someone whose body has all the integrity of a tea bag.

Life skills (M/F) (*See also* Reaching)

Each parent brings different skills to a relationship. These break down, fundamentally, into Woman: Earth Mother. Man: Donkey Boy. The important thing is to embrace your function, despite any perceived inequality.

You arrive at Manchester airport in a taxi. Slightly frazzled, clutching baby in car seat:

SHE: Pay the meter and get the suitcases out the car, I'll look after the tickets and passports.

YOU: (*Pavlovian like, you move towards the boot of the taxi, muttering under your breath*) Oh yeah, that's fair. I like your style, love, yeah. Don't mind old donkey boy's back . . . Don't want to get sweat stains on your velour leisure suit. *Grumble, grumble.*

SHE: (*gently applying sun cream to baby's head*) What are you saying?

YOU: Nothing. *Mumble, mumble, to self.* I like that, tickets and passports makes it sound like two things. I've only got *the* suitcases. *Grizzle, grizzle.* I'm surprised she doesn't rent me out. There must be a town in Spain in need of a dumb animal for a fiesta.

SHE: Don't forget his pram.

YOU: No problem. Don't tire yourself out, you've got thirty-seven different types of perfume to try on in duty free. *Whinge, whinge.* Then spend the next twenty minutes shoving various body parts up my nose, going 'smell this . . . smell that one, which one d'you like? There's one on my ear you haven't smelt'.

SHE: What perfume shop? Where? I need some new perfume. I'm bored with the ones I've got. I wonder if they've got any free moisturiser samples? You're sweating. Let me help. I'll hold your wallet.

NOTE It is possible that this is the reason why some women pack so much for holiday.

FRIEND: Nine pairs of shoes, for a weekend away. Isn't that excessive?

SHE: Yes, it is, but I can't decide. And don't forget I do have my own packhorse to carry it all.

FRIEND: Of course.

YOU: (*poking your head round the door*) *Hee Haaw* . . . all right, love. Taxi's here.

SHE: Great. Pop all the bags in the boot, put the bins out, and lock up will yer? I'll say goodbye to the cat.

YOU: Right you are, love.

Linea nigra

A darkened vertical line down the middle of the female abdomen, which appears in later stages of pregnancy to help the doctor find his way to the vagina. Medical training's not what it used to be. *See also* **Cutting the cord**.

Love (unconditional)

The strange bond that means when your child vomits all over you, you hoot with laughter instead of phoning an exorcist.

M

Man traps

Beware! If you want your baby to grow up with *two* parents, keep your defences up (*see also* **Zoos**). After the long haul of pregnancy, women are looking for reassurance and take pleasure in setting sly traps for you to fall into. Look out for innocuously delivered questions such as:

- I'm cuddlier now, aren't I?
- I really like *name of your ex here* for our daughter's name. What do you think?
- D'you think it's too early for me to wear low-waist jeans?

- If that's what you want to do, you go to the pub. I'll stay here with *your* crying child.
- In case there's ever an accident, we should give each other our PIN numbers.

Of course it is possible that your partner may forsake man traps altogether and merely exploit your failure to listen to most of what she says:

SHE: We're moving on Wednesday.
YOU: Are we?
SHE: Yes. I told you.
YOU: That's news to me.
SHE: I knew you weren't listening. Really, you never listen to anything I say.

SHE: We're married now.
YOU: We are not!
SHE: 'Fraid so. Last week. You signed the register, don't you remember?
YOU: Oh dear. I thought that was a birthday card.

Maternity bras

These are fascinating contraptions. Two clips and they're out. But it seems a cruel irony that the time they're most is the time when we're not allowed anywhere near them.

See Boo boos, 'IT'S NOT ALL ABOUT YOU ANY MORE', etc.

Maternity clothes

Unless you fancy blowing a few hundred quid to repair the damage, it's probably best to stifle any laughter that may emerge as you watch your partner struggle into a pair of unflattering elasticated corduroys. And if you do accidentally ask if she got dressed in the dark as she appears to be wearing a Mongolian yurt instead of normal clothes, be sure to get out of the way fast. Despite how she looks when she's lounging Wally the Walrus-like in front of the TV, propped up by several hundred **cushions**, with her swollen feet elevated on a heavily stocked biscuit barrel, she can move surprisingly quickly when she wants to.

Midwives

Although it is customary to thank the midwife for her help during the birth, resist the temptation to go out and wet the baby's head with her (especially while your partner's making a recovery). *See* **Zoos, Grievous bodily harm** etc.

Mistakes

- YOU: I've folded up the pushchair and put it in the boot.
  SHE: Great. Where's the baby?
  YOU: Ah. I'll be right back. *(to self)* That wasn't in the instructions.

- We have had the whole house redecorated: new sofas, silk curtains, Persian carpets, brand-new sound systems and widescreen TVs, the lot, everything we could need. It cost a fortune. Now we just have to wait for baby to arrive.
- So what story shall we read tonight, then? Vampire's Sabbath or Zombie Blood Quest?

See also **Wrong.**

Morning sickness

Apparently feels very similar in effect to alcohol poisoning (and funnily enough both are self-induced, although it's probably better to keep this observation to yourself). Can leave men thinking that women only really need us for two things: to get them pregnant and to hold their hair back when they are being sick.

Mother's Day

A very special event, which (conveniently) falls on different days in different countries. So, with enough air miles it's a great way to stock up on perfume, chocolates and bath salts.

Multiple births (twins, triplets, quads, etc.) – *see* Speed doting

Mums (post pregnancy)

Try not to be too clumsy around new mothers. They can be very touchy, due to stresses like lack of sleep, judgemental visitors, etc. Even accidentally waking the baby, for example (that she has just spent three hours trying to get to sleep), can lead to violent consequences, most probably with the nearest thing to hand:

FRIEND: How did he die?

SHE: With a breast pump. I clamped it to his face and sucked all the air out of his body cavities.

FRIEND: Didn't he run away?

SHE: No. I was wearing my slippers, he never heard me coming. He got a whiff of Johnson & Johnson and then it all went black.

FRIEND: How creative.

NOTE It is always worth pondering the question, 'Has having a baby changed me?' Then again, you may look in the mirror, see sick down your shirt, urine all over your trousers and poo under your fingernails and think, 'No. It hasn't changed me a bit.'

Musicals

Having a baby brings out the songsmith in all of us. In fact a casual observer may be forgiven for thinking that you and your baby are starring in a long-playing West End musical, as you conjure up cheery songs to take her through such routine tasks as eating stewed pears, removing an embarrassingly outgrown vest without taking most of the skin off her ears, and having a bath. Enjoy the process, safe in the knowledge that even when belting out an ad-libbed song like . . .

I'm having a bath with my mum. Doo da, Doo da.
I'm having a bath with my mum. Doo da, Doo da, day.

She washes my fingers, she washes my toes.
She washes my ears and she washes my nose.
She washes my belly and she washes my back.
She even washes my little bum crack.

I'm having a bath with my mum. Doo da, Doo da.
I'm having a bath with my mum. Doo da, Doo da, day.
(*repeat all day, every day until they are too embarrassed to bring friends back from school*)

. . . your work will still be better than one of Ben Elton and Andrew Lloyd Webber's efforts.

N

Names

The naming of your child is probably one of the most important decisions you make in its life. Something you might give just a few moments' thought to will follow a human being around for the rest of his or her life, influencing their personalities and chances of getting on in the world. So unless you already have one in mind, a family member or Internet password, etc., it's important not to rush it.

YOU: All right. What names have you got?
SHE: We've crossed out all the normal ones.

YOU: Well, let's do the un-normal ones. It's time to think outside the box.

SHE: OK. Here we go. Alvin.

YOU: Alvin? As in Stardust? Bit of a knobhead. Next.

SHE: Bronwyn?

YOU: Too Welsh.

SHE: Crispin.

YOU: Too poncey.

SHE: Darius.

YOU: Diarrhoea.

SHE: Osama?

YOU: Disneyland would be out. He'd never get through American customs.

SHE: Quentin.

YOU: Crisp? Behave.

SHE: Orlando.

YOU: Orlando? Fat smelly lad in grade four.

SHE: Enoch.

YOU: Too white.

SHE: Floyd.

YOU: Too black.

SHE: Giles.

YOU: Rhymes with piles. Next.

SHE: Phil?

YOU: Phil, Phile, Paedophile. No thank you.

SHE: Galen.

YOU: From *Planet of the Apes*? That's wrong on so many levels.

SHE: Fredo I like. Fredo Alexander?

YOU: Fredo Alexander Green? That spells FAG. Move on.

SHE: I can't, that's the lot. I give up. But we'll have to name him soon; Thingy's got his GCSEs next week.

YOU: What about Jack James Josh Jessica Mohammed. That covers all bases.

SHE: That's what I wanted in the first place.

NOTE It is also worth considering how your child's name feels in your voice when using some common expressions and likely phrases:

- Stephen, put your cousin the right way up.
- William, pass Mummy the bleach. No, the stuff in the lemonade bottle.
- Well, I'm sorry, Elmo – you'll just have to re-sit them.
- Do you have any idea where Chastity got the cider from, officer?
- It's *your* vomit, Pixiebell, you clean it up.
- No, Esmerelda. The correct question is, 'Do you want fries with that?'
- Have the girl's parents been informed of the pregnancy, Wayne?

Alternative names to call your baby:

- Nipple Breath
- Knuckle Sucker

- The Original Fanny Magnet (don't believe me? Try walking down the street with one)
- Gollum – the early years
- Young Winston
- Noddy Enthusiast
- Figure Thief

TIP 1 Some celebrities have named their children after the place they were conceived. Avoid this temptation. You'll only regret it in twenty years' time, when you have to explain the fad to your daughter 'Phonebox'.

TIP 2 Why not give your child an extra helping hand in life and give their Christian name a special twist – Lord, Doctor, Your Majesty – or, if you foresee a career in politics for them and expect to see their name on a ballot paper one day, how about 'None of the Above'.

Names your child should call you:

Father wish list: Sire. Pater. My better and elder. If you please, sir. The boss.

Get list: Dad. Spamhead. Oi, you. Old Man. Grumpy. Saddo. The Family Burden.

Mother wish list: Ma-ma. Mater. The light that melts my heart. My best friend.

Get list: Mam. Her. Why d'you have me then? She. The Purse.

Nappies

'Does my bum look big in this?' I'm afraid so.

> **NOTE At some moment, no matter how organised you are, you will run out of nappies. This is normal, even Germans do it. So when it happens, don't waste valuable time getting into a fight blaming each other, there will be plenty of opportunities for that on family holidays when you've had a few drinks and are looking for a perfect evening to ruin.**

Emergency nappies for every occasion:

- Shower cap, several *heavy flow* sanitary towels and a bicycle bungee.
- A roll of sellotape and a medium-sized Jiffy bag.
- Someone else's (very important, this) hand towel and a bulldog clip.
- Coffee filters and a pair of braces.
- A Tesco's carrier bag, dock leaves and some moss (suitable for getting caught out in the countryside).

Sorted.

Naughtiness

Are children capable of wickedness? Well, when you were a child did you ever lie at the bottom of the stairs with tomato sauce all over you and pretend you were dead to see if your parents cared about you? There's your answer.

Your parents return home to find you motionless at the bottom of the stairs:

DAD: Oh no. Our favourite child has died. Probably in an act of heroism, the world will never know. We've only got second-rate children left now.

SISTER: *(bristling)* I'll see if he's dead, Dad.

MUM: How?

SISTER: Like this.

She draws up a fulsome globule of saliva and catarrh from the back of her throat and gobs it into your face. Despite your best efforts, you blink and cough.

SISTER: It's a miracle. He lives. (*muttering*) Damn, I was going to have his bedroom.

NCT classes aka ante-natal classes

OK, we all know that there is no good reason for you as a man to be going to these classes, that you could learn more from a pamphlet or preferably a DVD, that if your partner was being reasonable and not the hormone-ravaged psychopath she has become she wouldn't make you go. But this is missing the point. These classes aren't for imparting useful information about the birth experience. Believe me, you aren't going to be at the birth, aimlessly offering out snacks, and suddenly be confronted by the scene:

DOCTOR: *(a hint of panic in his voice)* The baby's breeched. You there. Finger-food man. You've been to NCT classes. Put the vol au vents down and scrub up. Hurry.

YOU: *(trying to gulp down a Quaver)* Err, I wasn't actually paying attention. I felt a bit poorly and had to have a lie-down after seeing a line drawing of a dilated cervix. Cheesy nibble?

NOTE 1 Some people think NCT classes are merely an elaborate conspiracy/test set up by all the expectant mums to see if you and the other terrified male saps are committed to being a dad (*see* Man traps). Do go, drink their tea, snigger behind a biscuit with the other dads when told that a good way to bring on a late baby is to have sex, and accept them for what they are – your first experience of relinquishing your free will. Next stop, Pizza and Pingu evenings, stewed apple hair gel and traffic jams to the seaside on August bank holiday.

NOTE 2 Although lots of women find NCT classes are useful, the reality is that most men find them embarrassing. In particular the practice of performing a gentle back massage for their partners in front of other men:

CLASS TAKER: *(super-enthusiastic)* OK. I want all the women to form a circle on their hands and knees and let's have their partners kneeling behind them. I'll just dim the lights and put some whale music on.

There is a vague feeling of male discomfort in the room.

YOU: *(alarmed, under your breath)* Hang on, where's this going? This is how I got into this mess in the first place

CLASS TAKER: Now I want all you men to gently massage your partners' backs.

The men shift about more uncomfortably.

CLASS TAKER: Come on. These ladies have been on their feet all day carrying little one.

Each man half-heartedly starts stroking their partner's back.

CLASS TAKER: That's better. Super.

As each woman closes her eyes each man thinks:

Please somebody kill me.

And as the female noises of pleasure fill the room each man catches the eye of the other men in the room and mouths:

'We must never speak of this again! Mutually massaging my partner in front of other grown men? Lord sweet Jesus take me now.'

Night-time

You'll notice that you and your baby's attitude towards night-time differ somewhat. You may think you are sending baby off to the warm, gentle, fluffy land of 'beddy byes'. A place you wouldn't mind booking a fortnight in yourself (*see* **Zzzzz**). Some babies on the other hand – judging by the complaints – can't understand why you're locking them in a darkened room alone, with strange floating objects circling ominously overhead while the staring dolls of Death wait silently for them to drop their guard.

Nipples

Do women with large nipples have shortsighted babies? After all, it is a target. I'm just thinking out loud on this one. *See also* **Breasts**.

Normal behaviour (*see also* Parental paranoia)

Is my baby normal?

- Is she crying?

- Are you at the end of your tether?
- Do you look longingly at church doorsteps and wonder if you'll ever get a good night's sleep?

Then, yes, it is completely normal.

Nudge (The)

That heart-sinking prod in the back in the middle of the night that signals it's *your* turn to attend to the baby. Not to be confused with an offer of sex, which is altogether firmer and doesn't respond quite so well to being told to 'do it yourself'.

Numbers

Most women increase their use of dates and numbers by over 80 per cent from the first or second week of pregnancy: How many days late are you? How many weeks might you be? When's my due date? What trimester are you in? Have you had a 12-week scan? How many centimetres is it? What's its head circumference? Ten fingers and toes? How much weight have you put on? How long have you got to go? You'll need appointments every four weeks after week 12, every two weeks from week 32, and every week during the last three or four weeks. How many hours of contractions? How many centimetres dilated? What time was it born? What was his Apgar score? What was his weight? How many hours is he sleeping? How much weight has he put on? How many times does she wake in the night? How much sleep have you had? How long is he? How long did you get for maternity leave? How many mills is she taking? How much did it cost? What's AdultLine's number? When will it all be over? No, I want the EXACT time and day when it will be over.

O

Obesity (child) (*see also* Asthma)

It is a disturbing fact of modern life that many children are becoming obese. This is sad for the individuals concerned but does give the rest of us watching them come down the water slide a lot of fun.

YOU: *(enjoying a lazy afternoon with your newborn at Center Parcs, spying a large individual whizzing down)* Wow, look at Buddha go. He's pulling some G's, that boy. You're regretting those doughnuts now aren't you, sonny? Ooh, he's cleared the water, he's into the car park . . . I hope he's got third party, fire and theft.'

NOTE You may wonder what all the fuss is about fat children. After all, we're not putting them up chimneys any more.

Older parents

As a society we are having children later and later in life. So when is the right time to have a baby?

Hints it may be getting too late if:

- There is more chance of winning the lottery than the dads' race on school sports day.
- You say to your prospective partner: 'How do you want your eggs in the morning?' And she replies: 'Unpowdered, please.'
- Your hearing aid keeps interfering with the baby monitor.
- You are sharing nappies with your children.

Of course the longer you wait to have a baby the more chance there is that during those long days and nights reciting lullabies and having your arm slobbered all over, you *will* be tormented by knowing exactly what you're missing – dinner parties, holidays abroad, lie-ins, small amounts of luggage, clean carpets, etc.

Ominous

Upon hearing the following sentences, I suggest you make yourself scarce:

- If you fed him baby rice, why is the flour packet open?
- Where's the lid off my pen?
- You'd better come in here and give me a hand quick, it's gone all up his back.
- Right. I think you and I need to have a very long talk.

Onehandedness

babiesrequirealotofcarryingthereforeyouwillhavetoget usedtodoingeverythingonehanded*seealso***yoursexlife(if yougetmydrift)**whichmakeseatingyourdinnerwithout someonecuttingupyourfoodmakingyoufeellikeachildyour selfverydifficultandofcoursetypingespeciallycapitalisation andpunctuation

Overprotectiveness aka parental paranoia

When you find you've boarded all the windows up, sanded down every corner in the house, bubble-wrapped the budgie's beak and no longer allow anything into the house sharper than an aubergine, it is possible you may be going too far.

NOTE All your precautions will appear overcautious in comparison to your own childhood, when car travel

usually meant sitting on the parcel shelf or the dashboard (or on your dad's knee holding his cigarette so he could change gear), while teething on a piece of household asbestos.

See also Baby monitors, Am I ready for fatherhood?

P

Pamphlets

As the arrival of your new baby approaches, it is natural to want as much information as possible. As such, childbirth is to the pamphlet industry what binge drinking is to morning-after pill sales. Armfuls will be thrust upon you with every visit to the health centre.

Of special interest may be:

- How to bond with your baby – top tips from our friends at B&Q.
- Pregnancy and alcohol. Drinking for two now.

- Putting baby first, second, third and fourth and so on – learning to do without.
- 'It's different when they're your own' and other baby myths.
- Baby essentials – volumes 1–250.
- Camp beds – our guide to the top ten buys.
- Learning to love your parents again. A guide to free childcare.
- Home delivery? Now with free garlic bread and large bottle of cola.

Paternity leave

You will have to accept that men don't get much in the way of baby perks. (*See also* **Sex**, **Respect**, **Gifts**, **'IT'S NOT ALL ABOUT YOU ANYMORE'**, etc.) So, while women get six months' (paid) leave from work, men are deemed capable of getting over the whole thing in a couple of weeks, which as we all know is nowhere near enough time to improve your golf handicap. Self-employed people get bugger all, although if you claim to be a professional puppeteer or circus dwarf handler your child's clothes may become tax-deductible items. Hmm.

Pelvic floor exercises

Very important post-pregnancy workout aimed at countering the following common scenario:

SHE: Your organ feels small these days.

YOU: Hmph. Well, it's playing in a cathedral now, love.

SHE: Tetchy, are we?

YOU: Just a little tired. Sorry.

Phantom pregnancy symptoms

It's a curious feature of pregnancy that some men experience symptoms similar to their partner as she progresses through to childbirth – distended stomach, casual shoplifting, leaky breasts (never good in the baths after Sunday morning football). And it is a well-known fact that men deal with pain and illness on a different level from women:

YOU: I'm not well, love.

SHE: What's wrong now?

YOU: I've got terrible stomach ache.

SHE: Really? Try living with a basketball that's trying to get it on with your bladder 24/7.

YOU: *(not listening)* Yes, I think this is serious. This could be it. Feels like a tumour. Oh no. I'm getting weaker.

You sigh, then burp long and loudly.

YOU: Oh, that seems to have cleared it. Sorry, love. False alarm.

Philosophy

Having a baby shows you what's really important in life. Money. *See* **Kerching!**

Photos

Your collection of photos will increase dramatically once your baby arrives as you look to record for posterity such important action shots as:
Mum and baby in hospital. Baby with midwife. Dad with baby (out of focus, Dad's head cut off. Thanks). Baby's first hat. Baby's second hat. Third hat. Baby in hat and bootees. Baby's first pee. Baby's first pee over shoulder. Baby on back. Baby on back (in front of fire). Baby in bath. Baby yawning but if you squint it looks like he's smiling (he isn't). Sleeping baby. Sleeping baby in a different room. Sleeping baby in different room to the other different room. Sleeping baby in a carry sling. Sleeping baby in carry sling (head at funny angle). Mum and Dad with baby (finally). Grandparents with baby. Brothers and sisters with baby. Friends with baby. Baby with a dog. Baby almost sitting on the cat like a jockey (assisted). Walking baby (assisted). Sexy neighbour through a hedge (how did that get in there?). Baby with friend who doesn't want children (is that a fleeting look of discomfort or a hint of regret?). Baby with friend who hasn't had children yet (is that impatience or indigestion?). Baby with drunken uncle (tense moment that passes without incident. Move on but

log the feeling). Baby in oversized sunglasses (Elton John. Hilarious. Aren't babies fun?). Mum breastfeeding baby (cheeky). Baby nearly looking at the camera. Baby with hand over face, but it sort of looks like he's waving like a *real* person. Out-of-focus baby. Baby in car seat looking bemused. Baby next to Christmas tree. Baby surrounded by Christmas presents in the vain hope he may appreciate the occasion through osmosis. Baby lying on a cushion wearing a Christmas cracker hat – look in his eyes, he knows it's Christmas, you can tell. He's been here before this one (give it a rest, Gran). Grumpy baby. Grumpy baby again. Grumpy baby again. Very grumpy baby (OK, turn the flash off now). Exceedingly grumpy baby (I said turn the flash off). Crying baby (now you've done it). Crying baby 2. Crying baby 3. Howling baby. Screaming baby (put that camera near his face again and I'll shove it up your arse). Ely Cathedral. Clouds. A bus.

TIP Other people are notoriously dishonest when appraising children and babies. So why not crop a picture of Yoda (the weird-looking pointy-eared one from the *Star Wars* movies that isn't Liam Neeson) and put it in your wallet. Then when people say they've heard you've had a baby, pull out your wallet and say straight-faced, 'Yeah, that's him. Isn't he adorable?' and await their attempts to feign adoration.

Planning (pregnancy)

If you think your partner might appreciate travelling to hospital on the top deck of the night bus in slippers and dressing gown clutching industrial-strength panty pads and a toothbrush, while vicious contractions rack her body every couple of minutes making her drop her bus pass, then feel free to leave everything to the last minute. (*See also* **Spontaneity, Birth plan**)

Poo aka caca, poo poo, yucky mustard, etc

Prepare for your views to change. Babies have three main states: 1) pre-poo 2) pooing 3) post-poo. During pre-poo they can get unaccountably tetchy and you'll find yourself asking, 'What's the matter? Too hot? Too cold? Hungry? Want to be bounced on a knee? Fly through the air like a baby in the sky . . . ? Ah. That's what it was', and then the strange and ecstatic moment of victory, of production, arrives. The danger occurs in the transition from state 2 to 3: i.e., is it finished yet? No matter what preparations you make – nappy-changing zone, wipes, fifteen-minute wait, etc. – there will come a moment when it goes wrong, when even the modern nappy proves insufficient. In a way poos are like books – much nicer if they come out in instalments rather than one huge single volume. In this circumstance remember your first duty: Save the duvet!

Potty training

This is a big leap and calls for parents to celebrate each successful poo or wee in the potty. To begin with you can feign your delight but after a while, and a few accidents, this will become genuine. Don't let the celebrations get out of hand, though; a lap of honour holding the brimming utensil aloft is a recipe for disaster.

Prams

One of the most enjoyable aspects of becoming a parent is the opportunity to buy a new vehicle for the family.

YOU:	I like this one.
SHE:	Yes, but can it fold away one-handed? That's very important for public transport.
YOU:	It's got big tyres.
SHE:	What's its shopping storage like?
YOU:	Dunno, but look how easily you can pull a wheelie.
SHE:	Can you put the baby rear- and forward-facing for when it gets older?
YOU:	It's very shiny.
SHE:	Look, those are not the features that mark out a good pram.
YOU:	You're right. I was getting carried away. I'll ask if it comes with SatNav.

Pride

Many incidents will leave you with a warm glow, but that moment when your child breaks wind loudly and lengthily in a very quiet shop takes some beating.

Privacy

Two words. Dream on. (*See* **Spontaneity**)

Pyjamas

Aka daywear for mums.

Q

Quality time

Despite your new arrival, it is very important for both of you to make time for each other.

FRIEND: Are you getting any quality time these days?
SHE: Yes.
YOU: Surprisingly lots.
SHE: We had some last night, didn't we?
YOU: We did. Between three-thirty and three-thirty-two, I think it was.
SHE: We watched an advert together. It was lovely.

Questions

No doubt there are many questions running through your head as you enter new parenthood:

1 Will I be a good parent?
2 Will I make the same mistakes as my parents?
3 Who was Braxton Hicks, and was he a chronic asthmatic?
4 Which came first, the snack or the handy-sized Tupperware container to put it in?
5 Is that vice-like grip on my chest hairs the first sign of deviant behaviour?
6 Shall I burn my oh-so-flattering maternity clothes when I'm through with them or just cut them into shreds?
7 Why do people who snore always get to sleep first?
8 Why is judging my parents not as much fun as it used to be?
9 Will my child throw a huge party for me in years to come as a big thank you for bleeding me of my money, youth, health, hair and years of unpaid taxi services or will it shove me off to a care home as soon as I start eating my Sunday dinner with a spoon and my house starts to whiff of piss and biscuits?
10 When can I start letting myself go?

Quibbles

The name given to those enjoyable bite-sized arguments you have (that fill that gap before the main row at bedtime, *see* **Arguments**), which have recently changed from pre-birth morsels such as 'Chinese or Indian?', 'Red or white?' and 'Fetherlite or ribbed?' to 'Breast or bottle?', 'Caca or number twos?' and 'Hand job or nothing?'

Quips

Having a child expands your repertoire of jokes no end. Among my favourites are:

- Passing the baby over the supermarket counter and saying: And a baby, please.
- Boarding a bus: Two and a bit adults, please.
- 'Baby in boot'. Good when used with an empty car seat.
- 'Baby in care'. Ditto

REMEMBER Children say the funniest things. But only to their parents and grandparents. The rest of us are only interested in good video footage that involves a 'hilarious' personal accident/injury (preferably involving a puddle, some mud and a face). So if you don't have any, please keep their remarks to yourselves. *See* Am I a new parent bore?

R

Reaching

You may have noticed when baby arrives that along with emptying the nappy bin, making blatantly dishonest remarks about how good she looked in her maternity clothes and carrying your own body weight in luggage items (*see* **Life skills**), one of the domestic uses a woman has for a man, especially during this time of reduced mobility, is for getting things from the top shelves in the kitchen.

Huffing and puffing noises from the kitchen.

YOU: *(from the lounge, feet up, dangerously relaxed, making an offer you hope she refuses)* Want a hand, love?

SHE: No, you stay there and watch telly.

YOU: OK. Just shout if you need me.

You settle down into your chair pleased that you managed to convey that right balance of care with a garnish of reluctance in your voice.

SHE: *(entering the room at speed)* Of course I want a bloody hand . . .

YOU: Eh? But you said . . .

SHE: I can't do everything myself, you know.

YOU: Hey, don't worry. You've just got to ask. I'm not telepathic.

SHE: You don't need telepathy to know I can't look after a baby and make your tea.

YOU: Sorry. How can I help?

SHE: I need the pressure cooker. It's on the top shelf. I hate that shelf.

YOU: I can do that.

You reach on tiptoes and grab the cooker. The weight catches you by surprise.

SHE: Do you want a chair?

You humph at her impertinence while pulling several muscles. You refuse to show your distress. Doesn't she know she's with an alpha male? You pass her the cooker.

SHE: Thank you.

YOU: Anything else?

Please God nothing heavy.

SHE: Those place mats.

YOU: No problem. There you go, my little oompa loompa. Now off you go to your river of chocolate.

SHE: (*dreamily*) A river of chocolate, eh?

Reassurance

Pregnancy is a stressful time and everyone needs lots of reassurance, preferably in the form of cash gifts. Problems arise because some people (all right, women) are renowned for not saying what they want (*see* **The A–Z of Living Together**). So, if your partner says, 'Now we've got a baby, you don't have to bother buying me anything for Christmas' and you believe her, you may find you're seeing in a very, very chilly New Year. Of course, men should be grateful if they even get gifts. Most often we only seem to receive *nearly* presents. As in:

SHE: I was in Marks and Spencer's this afternoon.

YOU: Oh yeah?

SHE: Yeah. I got a lovely skirt and top.

YOU: Nice.

SHE: I *nearly* bought you a jumper while I was there, too.

YOU: (*resigned*) Oh right.

(*pause*)

SHE: I *nearly* bought you that CD you said you liked in HMV.

YOU: Hang on. What's all this *nearly*? Am I supposed to thank you for something I haven't received?

SHE: No.

YOU: Just checking.

(*pause*)

YOU: By the way I forgot to tell you, I *nearly* told the lads I couldn't make that trip to Amsterdam the weekend before the baby's due.

SHE: Don't push it. I'm hormonal.

Respect

You will leave the experience of childbirth with so much more appreciation for each other – you for her bravery and strength, she confident in the knowledge that when the chips are down you are a panicky individual prone to weeping.

Restaurants

It is a myth to think that your social life is over now that you have a baby. There are some fine restaurants out there waiting for you and your family to frequent: Happy Hippo, Wacky Warehouse. Ronald McTwats. Oh dear. Pass me the hemlock, and yes, I'll go large.

Rocking

Babies love to be rocked – no fulcrum should be overlooked. A good way to get babies off to sleep is to hum away while employing a simple side-to-side swaying motion (with the odd tapping on the back to give a soothing facsimile of mother's heart). However, do make sure you have a baby with you or you may be mistaken for someone who's given their carer the slip.

Role models

You both may be stressing about giving up drinking, gambling and any other vice which could look bad to your child. Before you do so, consider this: You can if you wish live your life so that your child looks up to you and wishes to emulate your achievements (or resents them), *or* you could live your life so that your child looks at you and decides there is no way he's going to make the same mistakes – the choice is yours. Surely it's kinder to leave a modest legacy that your child can easily surpass. 'I would have followed in my parents' footsteps but I couldn't find them!' That's what I'm saying, and I'm sticking to it. *See also* (**Guilt (Mother's), Am I ready for fatherhood?** etc.

Romance

It is important not to neglect your love life. Remember, when the baby is born, despite spending most of their day resembling a Jackson Pollock painting and smelling of caramel and uric acid, women still love a bit of romance. It's just a matter of degrees. Candles and massages are always a favourite, although why it always has to be with essential oils these days, I don't know:

SHE: You're very tense.

YOU: Yes, that's because I'm covered in oil next to a candle. Of course I'm tense. I'm jumpy, that's what I am. One wrong move and I'll go up like a wicker man.

Which hardly makes for a romantic outcome.

FRIEND: What happened to your boyfriend?

SHE: He was incinerated.

FRIEND: Really?

SHE: Yes, but he left a lovely smell of ylang-ylang, which I found rather calming.

NOTE For some reason the holy grail of accomplishments for a man to perform for his pregnant partner is a foot massage. One spontaneous foot massage with regular reminders (notes, prods, card on the anniversary, etc.) that you performed the act should put you in clover

for the duration of the child's life or at least until he's in long trousers. So hold back those feelings of servitude. Turn a blind eye to that bunion, the toenails the colour of Wensleydale and the callused heel. Ignore those damp little black sock fluff remnants between the toes, the clammy film of sweat and the gamey whiff . . . On second thoughts, I'm sorry, I just can't do it. Would some flowers from the garage be OK instead?

Romper suits

Those cute and comfy-looking all-in-one outfits that secretly make most adults think, 'I wish they did them in my size – in flannelette.'

As in:

SHOPKEEPER:	Nice outfit.
YOU:	Thanks. The missus got it me from Fathercare. Feel that, it's flannelette.
SHOPKEEPER:	Mmm, nice. In pink too. A daring colour for a man.
YOU:	Isn't it. But I think I manage to pull it off. D'you want to see me do a forward roll?
SHOPKEEPER:	Not just now thanks. Excuse me. (*over his shoulder*) Security.

(*See also* Clothes, etc.)

Routine

All books and family advice tell you to get your baby into a routine as early as possible, so always remember your six pre-bedtime B's: boob, bath, bed, bawling, battle, bribery!

S

Schools (primary)

Despite the temptation to relocate near a primary school to make life more convenient, don't get too close. The noise will turn you mad, as school rules dictate that kids must be let out every hour for ten minutes' synchronised screaming. In fact the sound from a primary school playground in full cry can be terrifying and you could be forgiven for thinking:

- Is there a lion loose in the school playground? Oh no, it's just a boy with his coat on back to front chasing people with a bit of bird poo on a lolly stick. Of course.
- Is it doomsday? Has the four-minute warning gone off?

No, it's a child with exceedingly chapped lips trying to join in a game of kiss chase. My mistake.

Separation anxiety – *see* How to wear your baby as a stylish brooch

Sex – BC, AD

You may notice that nowadays you are looking at your sex life using the traditional dating techniques, BC and AD. As in: BC – Before Child. AD – After Delivery.

YOU: It's been ages since we last had sex.
SHE: No, really. When?
YOU: 2006 BC.
SHE: Really. How do you know?
YOU: I marked it on the calendar. With a smiley face.
SHE: I wondered what that was. I thought it was the day I *nearly* bought you a car.
YOU: I'm going a bit mad. Last week I read that syphilis infections were up 70 per cent. I thought, Lucky sods. I dream of my teeth falling out and my knob dropping off.
SHE: Oh you do exaggerate.

TIP As mentioned before, it is said that to move the labour along, you should have sex or eat a curry –

although this may have been the choice/dilemma which got you into this situation in the first place.

NOTE We are often told that women like spontaneity in their sex life, although this may be difficult during late pregnancy – getting the winching gear into the house, putting hospital casualty on alert, etc., and of course spontaneity can lead to other problems:

YOU: I'm in a spot of bother.
FRIEND: Why's that?
YOU: The wife keeps saying I'm not spontaneous. So the other day, as she was reaching into the freezer, I thought, now's my chance.
FRIEND: And?
YOU: Now we're banned from Tesco's

The fact is as most men know, you can't just *have* sex – sex requires planning, graphs, bribes have to be induced, bladders have to be emptied, names memorised (that's a joke) and most importantly pets removed from the vicinity. There is nothing worse (actually there are several things worse, not least being tortured to death with an artichoke) than old kipper breath (cat) wandering in half way through your passionate encounter:

Sound of heavy purring. Which is worrying, because you've not heard your partner make that kind of noise before. Fortunately a cat's face emerges from around the door. There is a loud miaow.

YOU: Oh no. Not now.

SHE: What is it?

YOU: I knew I should have removed that slipper. The cat's here. Go away, Banjo.

The purring gets louder as the cat approaches your face.

YOU: Bugger off.

There is the noise of you blowing tail fluff out of your face.

YOU: Showing me your bottom is not helping.

The cat sneezes.

YOU: Oh a sneeze. Thank you. Very refreshing. Now go away. (*to your partner*) Hang on, love, he's on my back.

SHE: Go away, cat.

YOU: He's doing that drumming thing on my back. Treating me like a cheap galley slave. (*to the cat*) Not so fast. Slow it down. I can't go that fast. I'll never last. At least make me look good.

SHE: It's no good. Get off me. The moment has gone.

YOU: (*to the cat*) You did that. You're ruining me.

SHE: Leave him alone. He's just a cat.

YOU: (*muttering*) I knew we should have got a dog.

Sideways cuddle

Vaguely unsatisfying human-to-human contact that seems to be the only sort available in late pregnancy.

Sleeping on the job

What is wrong is to enjoy it!

Smiling

For a lot of people (all right, men), babies only really become interesting and adorable when they have become sufficiently developed to give us some positive feedback – usually by smiling or gurgling. This is because we are superficial and shallow and if this hasn't bothered you in life up to now, then there is nothing to worry about.

YOU: (*bending over the cot*) Who's Daddy's little boy? (*you tickle him under the chin*) Look, he's smiling. (*you beam pathetically*) Yes, I am special, aren't I? (*wiping a tear*) Validation at last.

NOTE You may notice babies will often smile directly at you then turn their face away quickly. This is because they're embarrassed that they don't have any teeth.

Snot (baby)

There will be buckets of it. In different colours, consistencies and flavours. (Oh dear, don't ask!) Not to be confused with **drool** which is clearer and less viscous. The differences are noted here only so you can contemplate how your life has come to this.

Spatulas

Along with fingernails, a useful device for quickly removing those stubborn spots of caca on your baby's bottom/leg/ear/wherever (it gets everywhere) that, to be fair, you've had your eye on for a few weeks but have been too knackered/tardy to remove before the grandparents/health-worker/new pal from the NCT class comes round to see how the little one is progressing. Just remember to wash all utensils before making breakfast.

> **TIP** Be careful picking off any unidentified stain/crust from your clothing/furniture/wall/ceiling/face with a fingernail and then tasting to see what it was. It might be food. Unfortunately with a baby around, it might also be food that has been eaten *before*. Do I make myself clear? Good.

Steamers

Important kitchen item for bottles, dummies and letter-snooping.

Stinginess

Undoubtedly one of the perks of your newfound status as a dad is your bona fide right to torment those around you with Dickensian miserliness. So get ready to enjoy harassing your family with several years of:

- Banging on the toilet door as you hear the loo roll being unwound with alarming speed – 'Two pieces in there. Do you hear? Your arse is only as big as a shirt button. Toilet paper doesn't grow on trees, you know.'
- Sneaking up on your child as they make lemon squash – 'That's too strong' – then getting a colour chart out of your pocket – 'You want down here – one part per million. No wonder you've got pimples.'
- Cutting the toes out of slippers – 'No one's going to see you, you only wear them in the house.'
- Sending your child to school with packed-lunch items from the 'no frills' range.
- Painting a permitted high water line round the bath.
- Assessing the tread-life on trainers with a coin.
- Insisting people walk round the edge of carpeted rooms.
- Leaving the plastic on sofas and car seats until you're

ready to sell it on, and then ladling your children out of the back on a sunny day.

Let the good times roll.

Support

It is vital that you support your partner, especially during late pregnancy and into active labour. This will manifest itself in different ways: comforting words of encouragement, making nourishing snacks, keeping an eye on her as she crosses the road now that pregnancy has made her a large, slow-moving target and, of course, only letting her bump-start the car if it's not raining, the road isn't slippy and she's got sensible shoes on.

> **TIP Remember: childbirth utilises the same muscles as pushing stools. (*See also* Involuntary bodily functions.) Too much empathy from Dad in the delivery room and you could be in trouble, so do remember to pack a bag with a change of underwear for yourself when your partner finally goes to the hospital.**

Swearing

Should you swear in front of your child? Well, it is a difficult one this. After all, it is a restrained parent who can board a busy bus with baby, shopping and (as an extra treat) lose a fingernail in the pram mechanism without resorting to the language of the Navy. However, it is probably best to resist the temptation for this simple reason – do you really want your bundle of love to be the one in school assembly who, when asked the name of the man on the cross, stands up and says: 'Jesus fucking Christ Almighty. And his mum's called Bloody Mary, get out from under my fucking feet.'

Swings

Fun as they are, remember: it's not the child who is tiring himself out, it's you.

Swivel eyeballs

Being cross-eyed is a charming affliction that affects most new-born babies. Or to use the common vernacular: one eye going to the shops, the other coming back with the change. Don't worry too much about it, as any associated anxiety must be offset by the baby's comfort in knowing that it's got four parents who love it.

T

Teething

Living with a baby can sometimes lead you to think a small beaver has moved in to the family home, as you survey your licked, chewed and gnawed prized possessions. Fortunately there are many teething rings on the market. Even more fortunately there are some other fine (and considerably cheaper) substitutes including a pair of old slippers, a length of four-by-two pine (six foot should get the busy little rodent through to puberty), or how about a squeaky bone from the pet shop? *See also* **Kerching!**, **Wrong**, etc.

Telling friends

One of the most enjoyable aspects of having a baby is breaking the news to friends and relatives, over and over and over again. And with the invention of photo mobile phones, you can show off to friends in other continents now too. Ah, progress.

Am I a new parent bore?

Try this simple test:

- You have your baby's photo on your phone, computer (screensaver *and* background), T-shirt (with a 'That's my boy' slogan) and are awaiting charges for spamming his image to everyone on your email list.
- Your conversational icebreakers include:

  She did something really cute today.
  How much sleep do *you* get a night?
  Will there be *other* children there?
  What are the schools like in your area?
  Nice pram.
  Do you have kids? No? Next!
- Your ears prick up when you hear strange words and expressions like 'Trimester', 'Formula', 'Car-seat head' and 'Free creche'.
- When you think of Mamas and Papas, you don't think 'California Dreamin''.
- When you look in the mirror, there is a weary yet self-satisfied phizog looking back at you.

If you nodded along to any of these in recognition, then the answer is probably yes. Or should that be 'Ah, bless'.

NOTE When your baby is finally born it is common for people to ask how much s/he weighed. The reason for this tradition is unknown.

FRIEND: So what did she weigh?

SHE: (*proudly*) 7lb 2oz.

FRIEND: Oh, what a shame. I only like 8lb 4oz babies.

Of course the main dimension that should be asked is how big his/her head was at birth as that surely is what is going to do the damage. Delivery of a 10lb pinhead is nowhere near as impressive as a 3lb baby with a head like a Chinese wok. Am I right, ladies?

Things . . .

Things that become harder to do when you are heavily pregnant:

- Persuade people that you're saving yourself for the right man.
- Find concealment behind a small tree when playing Hide and Seek.
- Take your knickers off in a sexy and provocative manner.
- Join a nunnery.
- Go out on the pull.
- Watch a cartoon without needing a slash halfway through.
- Receive fulsome approval from onlookers for staying on the Bucking Bronco the longest.
- See your feet.

Things that become easier to do now you're pregnant:

- Lounge about on the couch while everyone runs around trying to find your favourite food (that's a joke!). *See also* **Swinging the lead**.

Toddler

Colloquial term for the child who has learnt how legs work but has yet to grasp the fundamental laws of gravity.

Trimesters

Unusual word that means there is so much trouble in pregnancy that they've had to break it into three sections, although trimester two, with the arrival of the pendulous knockers, and trimester three, with those industrial-sized doses of happy **hormones**, do have wonderful compensations.

U

Ultrasound

Wonderful as it is to see the cross-section of that shadowy figure wobble about on the screen, nothing really prepares you for the real-life vision of the navy-blue rat that is thrust towards you as you are proclaimed a proud parent. (*See also* Firsts.)

NOTE It is a very special moment when you first see your baby's face, a face that never existed until you and your partner got together and mixed some DNA with a few glasses of a rather poky Shiraz. So take time to savour the moment before it dawns on you that, 'This

is the face that will one day be waving me off to the old people's home.'

CHILD: Bye, Dad. Thanks for the house.

YOU: But I'm still active. Don't send me off to live with all those nanas. I'm not ready for the nanas.

CHILD: We love you, Dad, but you've got to go.

YOU: Why?

CHILD: We've got some people coming round for Christmas dinner and we're a chair short.

YOU: Don't forget me.

CHILD: We won't, thingy.

Uncles/aunties

Originally referring to the parent's siblings, now a term attached to any passing stranger to imply 'trust'. As in:

- Now you be a good girl for Auntie Dawn while mummy tries this dress on. Does this come in a size 12, Auntie Dawn?
- Say hello to your Uncle Simon, he's not seen you before, has he? And a pint of lager, please, Simon.

Unfairness

That secret belief held by some women that despite all their love and sacrifices, their child will one day proclaim: 'Mum's always so stressed, too busy making my sandwiches, picking up my socks, ironing my clothes, reading me stories, driving me to school. She's never got any time for me. That's why I love my dad, he's much more chilled.' *See also* **Jealousy**.

Uses (baby)

As well as nail manicurist and wire stripper (*see* **Teething**), babies have lots of unexpected uses. For example, they provide the perfect cover for anyone wanting to talk to ducks, play with dolls or stick a 'y' or 'ie' on the end of real nouns: Bussy, doggy, horsey, fishy (unless you're an Australian or Auss-ie, in which case you don't need any encouragement).

V

Vanity

Babies, the ultimate vanity?

YOU:	I am so wonderful, the world needs two of me.
SHE:	That's right, love. Have you been in work all day with those cappuccino chocolate marks on the corners of your mouth?
YOU:	I suppose I must have done. No wonder I never get promotion.

Village

It is said that it takes a village to bring up a child, although there's always the chance it may turn out to be the idiot. Not to be confused with leaving your baby in the care of a group of men wearing Native American, construction worker and New York cop costumes singing Y.M.C.A.

Video cameras

A video camera is essential for the birth. The only problem will be what you shelve the footage under: family, comedy, romance, adult or horror? Or perhaps all of them.

Visitors

People love babies. So you must expect visitors. Don't worry, visitors are great. They bring gifts. Champagne, frankincense, myrrh, sheepskin booties (well, they do if you drop enough hints). And of course now there is no need to concoct elaborate lies when you want to get rid of them, simply open up a conversation along the lines of:

YOU: Look, she'll be desperate for you to stay longer (you being her most favourite friend and everything, lick,

lick, stroke, stroke) but you mustn't let her persuade you. She's putting a brave face on it but she's very tired and the doctor says she needs all the rest she can get *(you pull them conspiratorially closer)* to heal the stitches in her, I think it's called the perineum.

FEMALE FRIEND: I've heard of that. No problem. *(she inadvertently and regretfully pictures the image)* You know. I wish you hadn't told me that.

NOTE If you listen to your partner (try it, it's fun), there is a pecking order with visitors. Interfering with this secret hierarchy could leave you with family problems for years to come:

Inner Circle: Blood relatives, best friend (check to see who they may be this week), those with expensive gifts.

Outer Circle: Work colleagues, school friends, NCT class women.

Very Outer Circle: Strangers, any of *your* friends.

In the hospital a few moments after the birth:

YOU: *(jovially)* You'd better wipe that goo off the kid and cover yourself up, love, My mate Dave's just texted to say some of the lads from the pub are on their way. I said it'd be OK.

SHE: Here? Now?

YOU: Yes. Get in before the rush, as it were.

SHE: Tell him you'll meet them in casualty. It'll save an ambulance trip.

YOU: What are you doing with that breast pump?

Volvos

It's just a matter of time. *See also* **Father blues**.

W

Weight training

There is no excuse for either of you to neglect your fitness regime after having a baby (*see* **Man traps**). In fact having a 7lb(ish) lump around the house makes for a perfect weight-training aid, one that symbiotically gains in weight as your strength improves, too. Three reps of 'Fly Through The Air, Supersonic Boy', two reps each of 'Peek A Boo' and 'Rock A Bye Baby', finishing off with a five-minute cool down of 'Giddy up, Horsey' should keep you in tip-top **yummy mummy** condition, especially if you stick with it till he's fifteen.

Who's the daddy?

It has been medically proven that babies naturally resemble their father when they are born. The reason for this is supposedly to stop Dad leaving the cave if he feels the child isn't his – interestingly, a few weeks later the baby begins to adopt some of Mum's features, when they discover who the *real* boss is.

NOTE Sadly some babies don't even manage to look like anyone from their own species when newborn – the nearest thing in the animal kingdom they resemble would be a tortoise pulled from its shell. Do not make this observation out loud. ***See also*** **Birth (The)**

Wombs

A quick visit round a labour ward, seeing all those newborn babies with their hair sticking up, will make you wonder whether the human womb is in fact made of nylon.

SHE: Her hair keeps sticking up. I've tried everything. What should I do?

FRIEND: Have you tried rubber boots and an earthing rod? Failing that, give her a rub and you'll find she's invaluable for picking up dust and fluff around the home.

SHE: Ta. I'll let *Woman's Weekly* know.

Working together

The key to successful parenting is working as a team. Much like a shepherdess and her dog.

Wrong

- SHE: Is that a new teething ring he's chewing?
  YOU: No, it's one I found in the park. Don't worry, I wiped it first.
- Baby as a back scratcher.
- Baby as a Trojan Horse to gain entry to the women's changing rooms.
- Leaving baby in the car with a gerbil water dispenser and a little sign saying 'Gone to play slot machines in pub – back in five minutes.'
- 'The flat lease forbids pets, so let's have a baby.'
- 'That £250 Government child trust fund will pay for a hooker to pop his "cherry" when he reaches sixteen.'
- 'So, childbirth. Did it make your fanny hurt?'

X

Xmas (first)

Along with walks in the park singing inane nonsense, **cupcaking** and Sunday morning raspberry belly farts, having a baby means you can enjoy Christmas again without accusations of childishness. Do not expect too much from your first Christmas though:

Common first Christmas errors:

- Hanging baby in a stocking for a photo opportunity without checking the strength of the drawing pin.
- Wearing tinsel around your boobs during feeding: 'It's his Christmas dinner too.' (But only if you leave

it on when next-door neighbours come round for a drink later.)

- Drunkenly taking him within reach of the Christmas tree, forgetting those fingers can without warning whip out octopus-like with an iron grip:

YOU: (*in suitably sing-song voice*) Here it is. These are the decorations. (*over shoulder*) Just a small Bailey's. Aren't they lovely, and these are the . . . hey, oh God, he's got the tree. Somebody help. Don't pull it, son. Let it go now. Love? Please. Somebody?

SHE: You stupid sod. You're too close.

YOU: It's OK. Don't panic. Not in the mouth, boy. They're electric lights. They don't like being sucked. Let's have the light bulb out of your mouth, son. Don't squeeze the glass bauble. It's glass. It doesn't like being . . .

SHE: Medic!

NEIGHBOUR: Is the baby hurt?

SHE: No, but the father's going to be.

- Dressing him/her as an elf. Ever.

TIP Although the old adage 'Christmas is for kids' is mostly true, no matter how drunk you are, remember it is morally dubious to offer to play a game of Operation with that annoying nephew, then suggest that you wire it up to the 240-volt mains to make it a bit more interesting.

Xylophone

For many a child, their first musical instrument (and as such too much of a temptation for any author compiling an A–Z book): if you ignore the improvised beaker and table-top drum kit, or indeed the cat, which he occasionally tries to play like the bagpipes. Xylophones are usually given by people who don't have children and don't live next door to any.

YOU: (*having a good moan*) And some fuckwit bought him a xylophone. Now I wake every morning to the theme tune of the Chinese version of *Psycho*, followed by an hour of him doing an impression of a wind-chime salesman falling down a lift shaft.

FRIEND: I bought him that.

YOU: Oh. Well he loves it. Plays with it for hours.

Y

Yoga

It is said that a good way to get your figure back after pregnancy is to practise yoga. However, do be careful when performing advanced positions. Geri Halliwell, a well-known yoga enthusiast, has developed a stubborn yoga injury that you may have noticed. She's got her head stuck up her arse. *See also* **Bendy mums**, **Relaxin**, etc.

Yummy mummies

The modern phenomenon of well-turned-out, 4×4-driving mothers in sexy gym wear and jogging shoes who have equally colour-matched offspring. Not to be confused with slummy/scummy mummies who also wear tracksuits but prefer to match them with white stilettos and a visible washed-out grey thong while out scouring the estate for their next breeding partner. *See also* **Sad dads**.

Yes

The correct answer to ANY offer of childcare duties. Don't be proud. *See also* **Babysitters**.

Z

Zebedee

Annoying little bugger from *The Magic Roundabout* with a dodgy moustache who tells us all to go to bed . . . If only it were that easy, you springy-arsed twat. Enough, Jeff. *See* Zzzzz.

Zero

Chances over the next few years of:

- Anyone wanting to sit next to you on public transport.
- Completing any journey with your clothing and dignity intact.

- Pulling off a carefree, louche act.
- Lying in bed late on Sunday morning, freshly secreted sleep mucus glinting in the morning sun, declaring, 'I haven't got a care in the world . . .'
- Engaging in wild, abandoned sex for the next few years without feeling obliged to keep one ear cocked and a slipper to keep the door ajar.
- Waking up (of your own accord) and the first thing on your mind not being, 'Bloody hell, I've got a kid.'
- Wanting any of this to change.

Zoos (for fathers) (*see also* Bitterness, Dressing up as superhero and climbing national monuments, Father's Day, etc.

Unless you enjoy looking at baboons' bottoms every other Sunday (nothing wrong with that of course), with the odd half-term thrown in if you meet the maintenance payments promptly, it might be a good idea to keep any comments about Mum's emerging bingo wings and jelly belly to yourself. And if things do go sour, avoid the temptation to draw analogies to your estranged partner when observing the displayed animals: 'That camel looks grumpy; how is your mother?', 'My God that chimp has the morals of a common tart; how is your mother?', 'Shall we go and have a look at the leeches and vampire bats?', because hey, no one likes a bad loser.

Zzzzz aka sleep (*see also* Getting baby to sleep, etc.)

You may notice that you are looking upon your partner with suspicion in your eyes these days:

YOU: Did you sleep? You slept. You selfish swine.

SHE: I did not. When?

YOU: In the chair. I heard you snoring.

SHE: Snoring? I haven't snored in months. I dream of snoring. How dare you say I was snoring? I hover in a half-sleep. Neither dead nor alive. Incapacitated, not refreshed. How can you say I snore?

YOU: Well I heard something.

SHE: Don't make me get my breast pump.

YOU: Sorry. It must have been the cat.

Or

YOU: . . . and eleven pints of milk please.

SHOPKEEPER: Newborn baby?

YOU: How d'you guess?

SHOPKEEPER: This is a car showroom.

YOU: Sorry. I'm a little tired.

SHOPKEEPER: Not getting enough sleep?

YOU: Mustn't grumble. I got twenty minutes in last week.

SHOPKEEPER: Where's your baby?

YOU: With his mum. I'm just killing time.

SHOPKEEPER: Is there anything else I can help you with?

YOU: (*looking both ways*) Yes. Can I have a lie down in the back of your Ford Focus? I'll pay you. And there's an extra fiver if you don't mention it to the missus.

Acknowledgements

My heartfelt thanks go to Fiona, Orlo and Fiona (our midwife); to Nick Herrett, Simon Munnery, Lee Stuart Evans for their invaluable help and feedback; and of course to Antonia, Addison, Joe, Kirsteen and Katie Phillips for their wonderful support.

THE A–Z OF LIVING TOGETHER

A Survival Guide

Jeff Green

With a foreword by Jo Brand

What happens when those two most incompatible of creatures – the human male and the human female – settle down for a life of togetherness and arguments about the toilet seat? Award-winning comedian Jeff Green bravely sets out to discover the truth. Why is 'Wow, you're a fantastic cleaner' not considered a compliment? And what *is* it about women and candles . . . ?

Along the way he offers

- helpful advice: why you shouldn't cheer when your partner says, 'I'm not angry, I'm disappointed'
- handy tips: ways to avoid becoming broody – get up every hour throughout the night and burn £200
- and essential buys: see exercise equipment and other places to hang wet washing'.

Whether you're hopelessly coupled or blissfully single, *The A-Z of Living Together* has all the answers you need. Because it's not just men who behave badly . . .

'One of Britain's very best observational comics'
Guardian

sphere

THE A–Z OF BEING SINGLE

A Survival Guide to Dating and Mating

Jeff Green

Ah the singer life. The blind dates, the [illegible] sleeping in the [illegible], the [illegible] In his hilarious new book, Jeff Green offers [illegible] advice on how to find [illegible] [illegible]

Also includes:

- [illegible]
- [illegible]
- [illegible]
- [illegible]

[illegible]

sphere

THE A–Z OF BEING SINGLE

A Survival Guide to Dating and Mating

Jeff Green

Ah, the single life. The blind dates, the guiltless sleeping in the starfish position, the 'table for one in a draught, please'. In his hilarious new book, Jeff Green offers practical advice on how to find love, or failing that how to pretend you've got a significant other half. For women: Leave the fridge door open for no reason. For men: Wash your towels. And if you've just been dumped, Jeff shows how you can reach 'closure', otherwise known as uncompromising REVENGE.

Also includes:

- Great chat-up lines for the older lover: 'Did you break a hip when you fell from heaven?'
- Beauty tips for dates: How to look twenty years younger? Stand further away.
- Things not to say on a first date: 'Would you like to see my shrine to the others?'
- And at last, the truth about what women really want*.

If you're in a couple, this book will remind you why your own situation is – just about – worth tolerating. And if you're happily single, follow Jeff's advice and you're guaranteed to stay that way . . .

*everything

sphere

Other bestselling titles available by mail:

☐ The A–Z of Living Together	Jeff Green	£6.99
☐ The A–Z of Being Single	Jeff Green	£6.99

The prices shown above are correct at time of going to press. However, the publishers reserve the right to increase prices on covers from those previously advertised without further notice.

sphere

SPHERE
PO Box 121, Kettering, Northants NN14 4ZQ
Tel: 01832 737525, Fax: 01832 733076
Email: aspenhouse@FSBDial.co.uk

POST AND PACKING:
Payments can be made as follows: cheque, postal order (payable to Sphere), credit card or Switch Card. Do not send cash or currency.

All UK Orders	**FREE OF CHARGE**
EC & Overseas	25% of order value

Name (BLOCK LETTERS) . . . .

Address . . . .

Post/zip code: . . . .

☐ Please keep me in touch with future Sphere publications

☐ I enclose my remittance £ . . . .

☐ I wish to pay by Visa/Access/Mastercard/Eurocard/Switch Card

Card Expiry Date ☐☐☐☐ Switch Issue No. ☐☐